Language**assistant**

Clare Lavery

Acknowledgements

The author is grateful to Muguette Moreau, Rita Legoux and all her former colleagues at the CES Emile Verhaeren in Bonsecours for making the year in classes bilingues so enjoyable. This positive experience led to a fruitful career in EFL. Many thanks to the fourth-year students at Queen Mary and Westfield College University of London and at Newcastle University for their time chatting about their year abroad. Thanks also to all those assistants who sent the author questionnaires during their assistantship in 2001. Your comments and thoughts were detailed, helpful and very instructive. Finally, special thanks to Kate Merrett whose encouragement and practical support made the writing of this resource book possible.

The poem 'A bad habit' by Michael Rosen, from *You Tell Me* by Roger McGough and Michael Rosen (Kestrel, 1979) © Michael Rosen 1979, is reproduced by kind permission of the publisher.

'Smoke-loving girl blues' from *Get Back, Pimple!* (Puffin 1997) is reprinted by kind permission of the author, John Agard, c/o Caroline Sheldon Literary Agency.

'Every Breath You Take' words and music by Sting © 1983, reproduced by permission of G M Sumner/EMI Music Publishing Ltd, London WC2H 0QY. Permission granted for the territory of the World.

'My Generation' by Pete Townshend © 1965 Fabulous Music Ltd, Suite 2.07, Plaza 535 King's Road, London SW10 0SZ. International copyright secured. All rights reserved. Used by permission.

'Twenty Flight Rock' words and music by Ned Fairchild and Eddie Cochran, © 1957 American Music Incorporated, USA. Campbell Connelly & Company Limited, 8/9 Frith Street, London W1. Used by permission of Music Sales Ltd. All rights reserved. International copyright secured.

'I Say a Little Prayer' words by Hal David, music by Burt Bacharach © 1966 Blue Seas Music Incorporated/Casa David Music Incorporated, USA. Universal/MCA Music Ltd, 77 Fulham Palace Road, London W6 (50 per cent)/ Windswept Pacific Music Ltd, Hope House, 40 St Peter's Road, London W6 (50 per cent). Used by permission of Music Sales Ltd. All rights reserved. International copyright secured.

Photography credits

Mark Hakansson, Andy Huggett, Jorge Relancio, Norio Suzuki, Liba Taylor

Contents

Module 2 Spoken English

Unit 4 – Oral practice

Unit 5 – Conversation and discussion with texts

Unit 6 – Speech work

Module 3 Teaching Aids

Unit 7 – Visual aids

Unit 8 – Listening and speaking

Unit 9 – Games

Module 4 Content and resources

Unit 10 – Cultural content

Unit 11 – Literature and the media

Unit 12 – Building a resource bank

Foreword

I am delighted that with this resource book the British Council is lending its support to the longstanding and successful language assistants programme.

Since the inception of this programme in 1904 many thousands of young people have benefited from this unique opportunity to spend an academic year in a foreign school. Equally, the students and teachers in the schools abroad have gained much from the presence of an English language assistant in their midst.

In the international community of the twenty-first century the value of this human contact has become more important than ever. The year abroad naturally enhances linguistic skills, but at the same time offers other valuable benefits, whether these are learning how to manage people, understanding how to operate in a different cultural context, or acquiring new communication and presentation skills.

This resource book has been specially designed for language assistants. It is practical and easy to use, and will support, inform and help you in your teaching. I hope too that it will contribute to your enjoyment of the experience and stand you in good stead for your future career, whether within the teaching profession or in the wider world of business and commerce.

Martin Davidson CMG
Chief Executive

Martin Davidson, British Council

Unit 1 Interpersonal relationships

What is the role of an assistant?

You may be asked what you will be doing in your year abroad. Perhaps you have had the opportunity to talk to former assistants but are still not any clearer about what you will be expected to do in your host school or schools. Rest assured that there is no set way to be an assistant and that schools abroad have evolved their own interpretation of how best they will use you. Some assistants complain that the schools don't know what to do with them. Look on this as an opportunity to make the most of the job and to develop a role for yourself.

In theory an assistant is there to help language teachers with their classes but should not be expected to teach a whole class alone. In practice, any of the following situations described by assistants across Western Europe in 2001 may apply to you.

Different roles

Team teaching
pp 5–8

- *'I take half the class for conversation whilst the teacher does a reading comprehension with the others. We alternate each lesson and it works well.'*

- *'I take the whole class for discussions while the teacher marks books at the back of the class.'*

- *'I take small groups of five or eight students who need extra help into another room for forty-five to fifty minutes.'*

Dealing with large classes
p 19

- *'I teach whole classes completely on my own and am left to my own devices.'*

- *'I am shared by all English teachers who give me little notice as to when they will need me in their lessons.'*

- *'I am always in classes with teachers who sometimes refer to me for help with pronunciation or explanations of difficult vocabulary. I am not allowed to run activities myself and get a bit bored.'*

It helps to keep an open mind regarding what you will be expected to do. Nevertheless you also need to be fairly firm with your host school if you find they are giving you far too many hours or classes with the full responsibility of a teacher. The first few weeks are crucial in establishing your role in the school and your relationship with the teachers and the students. You may have to negotiate your timetable, you may be asked to find your own teaching materials and you may find yourself coping with large classes for the first time. Despite initial hiccups which require diplomacy and tact, most assistants go on to enjoy what can be a very rewarding year.

Initial contacts

The more you know about the school and teachers before you go, the better. If you are given the contact name and address of the previous assistant then follow this up. Ask specifically about classes, types of material needed, teachers and timetables. The assistant may even have left behind teaching material which could be useful for you. Do not be put off by a negative account – each individual will view places differently and will strike up a different rapport with the school. Two assistants in the same situation react differently. One assistant given large classes by himself remarked: *'I enjoyed the freedom of doing what I wanted with them'*, while another in a similar situation remarked: *'They leave me to my own devices and skive off in the staff room while I blunder along with whole classes'*. In other words, one man's hell is another man's heaven.

Establishing a rapport with students
pp 14–15

The school culture
pp 12–13

Before leaving the UK
pp 126–7

Collecting resource material
pp 127–9

Useful tips

- **Write to or telephone the school** and its English teachers as soon as you can, preferably before leaving the UK.

- **Prepare a list of questions** to help yourself collect resources (see below) and to give you an idea of the types of classes and teaching you might encounter.

- **Ask teachers about** the levels of English of some classes you might encounter. You can then consult ELT textbooks for that level and age range in your local bookshops or at university to get an idea of how much they might be able to do. This will also help you to choose material to take with you. This can be important when you arrive laden with interesting newspaper articles on teenage issues but find the teens in your classes cannot cope with authentic articles because their language level is too low.

3

What to ask schools and teachers before and/or on arrival

Teaching information

- likely timetable

- age ranges you will be dealing with (some people find themselves spread over two or more schools)

- number of years students have been studying English (does not always indicate their level)

- levels of English you will meet and the textbooks used (try to get copies, even if just on loan for a weekend)

- whether you will be team teaching, taking small groups alone or dealing with whole classes alone

Visual aids
pp 68–79

- types of facilities and equipment available for your use, e.g. tape recorder, CD player, video machine, photocopying facilities, etc. (It's no use taking a pile of videos if there is no machine! If you can't have access to photo-copying you will have to work around that.)

- availability of card, paper, chalk, pens and other materials for making visuals and teaching material. In primary schools there may be a class stock. Be careful not to put a strain on your own pocket!

Administrative information

- your point of contact in school for timetable, pay and any problems

- your responsibility if a teacher you team teach with is ill – are you expected to hold the class?

- procedures regarding illness if you can't get to work

- procedures to follow if a pupil falls ill during one of your lessons

Discipline problems
pp 21–3

- the types of punishment you are allowed to give or procedures for very unruly students (Can you send someone out of the class? Where to?)

- procedures regarding registers of attendance (Do you keep one?)

- records of work (Are you expected to make a formal note in an official work book to record what you have done in your class after each lesson?)

Establishing a working relationship with teachers

You will be required to work as a team with the teachers in your schools but it is very much up to you to get this team established. It might help in your introductory letter or call to a teacher to show willingness to collaborate. For example, some teachers may not have had an opportunity to visit the UK for a long time. Would they like you to bring anything like magazines, a specific newspaper or some brochures? Show a willingness to work enthusiastically with them to break the ice. Bear in mind that they too may be unsure of how you might work together or insecure about their own English when faced with a native speaker. This can be compounded when the native speaker is closer in age to their students and arrives with a mission to woo the students as a friend. Your primary role is that of an assistant to the teaching team and for the duration of your job you are a member of staff. The students may be close in age, which means that you may well be able to empathise with them, but you are not there to set yourself up as a 'mate'. They will like you if they enjoy their lessons and if you are well prepared. It is also counterproductive to see your role in competition with the English teachers. You are a member of the staff and will be accepted and welcomed by them if you arrive with an enthusiastic, but professional, approach to the job.

On arrival the assistant is sometimes thrown by the lack of a welcoming party. Many assistants join the school after the start of term and are launched into an already buzzing staffroom filled with many teachers who will not be in your subject area. If they ignore your presence, it is not always through rudeness. You will have to find the person in charge of you, ask about your timetable, seek out English teachers and make things happen. At college, students are given information, timetables organised for them and tutors are there to support you in your studies. In most schools you are in charge of your own situation and you make things happen. This comes as a shock to some. You will need help but you must choose the right time to ask for it. An average teacher, with a full timetable and lots of preparation and marking to do, as well as other commitments, has little time and has to fit a lot in. Stopping teachers ten minutes before they have to rush off to a lesson or while they are using their only twenty minutes that day to sort out next week's exams can mean that their response to you is less than enthusiastic. Don't take their apparent briskness personally. Be patient and sensitive to this and make formal arrangements to speak to them when convenient. Ask teachers when it is most convenient for them to stop and chat about work. You will have to use this time with the teacher carefully, so

Establishing a rapport with students pp 14–15

Planning discussion work with teachers p 46

Being a willing pronunciation model for teachers to use p 65

5

prepare questions before and keep to specifics. If you work well together a relationship will blossom, but it can start off on the wrong footing if you arrive expecting attention. They might not even realise what type of help you require, so be very clear and don't hide your uncertainties.

Planning your work with teachers

Useful tips

- **Establish a timetable that suits both of you**. Be flexible. Take an early morning class if this means you have no classes on Friday afternoons and can go away for weekend trips. Some schools are rigid in giving you a timetable but others will be more open to compromise.

- **Take responsibility for your timetable**. If no one comes forward to get a timetable organised for you then approach teachers and suggest that you could be of use to them. Can you listen to students read aloud for their oral exams? Would it help the teacher if you practised vocabulary with some of the learners in their classes? Think of ways to be of service instead of waiting in the staffroom to be asked.

- **Protect yourself from exploitation or being over-stretched**. If your role is an itinerant assistant to be spread across all teachers then try to negotiate some basic guidelines so you can at least plan a bit ahead. You cannot hang around the school all day waiting to be used at the whim of teachers, or worse, as a cheap supply teacher.

  – Be flexible for lessons at short notice (an hour?) where you will be with a teacher who is doing the main teaching and using you as a helper.

  – Insist on at least twenty-four hours' notice for a class which you must take alone, so you have time to prepare.

  – Make it clear that you are not a supply teacher, but be flexible if a teacher you are working with falls ill unexpectedly. Insist on being given worksheets or instructions in these cases.

Oral exams
p 66

Pair revision fillers
p 31

Dictation
p 84

Jumbled stories
p 43

Large pictures
p 74

Revision fillers
p 100

Pronunciation fillers
pp 59–60

- **Make a link between your work and the teacher's work**. Once assigned a group to take by yourself try to get a rough idea of what their main teacher will be covering each two-week period. The teacher might specifically request you to practise something covered recently (e.g. the conditional tense) but in a different way. If there are no specific requests, bear in mind that your role is to facilitate language use so you need to do activities that encourage learners to activate the vocabulary and language recently studied. If you note that the textbook covers ways of giving advice, set up a reading and role play where students have to give advice to each other. If they have done numbers above 100 devise a numbers game for your lesson. Always keep track of what they are studying even if you are asked to do something different.

- **Talk through your plans with teachers**. It is not always clear how much teachers want to know about your lessons, but you need a sounding board. Request an official appointment (once a fortnight, once a month) to discuss the types of things you will do with classes. Ask for advice, with equipment, difficult pupils, etc. Show you value the teacher's opinion and do not let any worries get out of control. The amount of co-operation teachers expect also depends on their previous experience of assistants and on their work at school. In some school systems each individual teacher works alone, rarely co-ordinating with colleagues. What you need and what you are proposing might be new and might not occur. Be patient and persevere.

Controlled oral
practice
pp 36–41

Games and
role play
pp 92–101

Feedback
on errors
pp 29–34

'My school is a huge one – Gymnasium, Realschule and Hauptschule in one building and a Grundschule about three minutes' walk away. I asked the secretary for a list of English teachers, got their timetables and went on the hunt! Basically I asked loads of people if they taught English and if they could use me at all. I think that's basically the problem – no one knows I'm there.'
Susannah McDonnell, Assistant in Germany.

Team teaching tips

If you are in a school that puts the assistant in a class with a teacher then you are forced into a relationship which needs collaboration. Team teaching presupposes an element of mutual respect and works well if planned and guidelines are established.

Remember that your primary role is to assist so don't try and take over teaching or resent being second fiddle to the main class teacher.

Speech work
pp 56–67

Remember that you are valuable as a resource of authentic knowledge on all things English. Don't worry if you feel like a human dictionary or a pronunciation model. These are useful functions in a language class and the teachers will want to exploit your knowledge. Respect the teachers' knowledge of your language system too.

Keep criticism and contradiction of the teacher to the staffroom. If the teacher corrects you in front of students and you feel it is unjustified, air your grievance in private. Explain that these discussions about your accent, use of language or approach are interesting and a learning experience for both of you. In class these discussions confuse students.

Try to find out what is expected before the lesson. If a reading activity is going to be covered, go through it beforehand and practise explaining words that students might ask about. If some oral work is to be done, anticipate pronunciation work and practise your intonation.

Request and offer feedback after a lesson together. Ask for help from the teacher or suggest other ways you could be useful. Try and keep the lines of communication open so your teamwork develops instead of falling into a routine. There's nothing worse than spending hours sitting at the back, seething or bored, not knowing when you are to be used.

Always follow the lesson closely. If you are not taking half the class but waiting until you are needed, keep up with what is happening. Try to watch the students and teacher actively. Use it as observation time, not nap time!

'My job as an assistant is very much to assist rather than teach. New vocabulary does (and should) crop up in every lesson, but from a grammar point of view the teachers are likely to have a much greater knowledge of English than the mother tongue speakers. For example, I can say that a piece of grammar is wrong, but I turn to the teacher for an explanation as to why it is wrong.' **Simon Cooper, Bergamo, Italy. Assistant in a liceo scientifico.**

Learning approaches
pp 13–14

The observation period

It is advisable for all new assistants to have a week or two just sitting in on lessons and observing students. Unfortunately not all schools allow for this, but be assertive and explain how you need this time to get to know the classes and the types of teaching expected of you. This period of observation can be extremely valuable if you use it wisely. Watching the teachers can give you great insight into the types of learning students are comfortable with or accustomed to, and also the potential difficulties that the students have with the language. You can also note the potential troublemakers and the dynamics of each group. Learn how the teachers deal with insolence, rowdiness or lack of interest. After observation ask teachers about school policy regarding discipline. This observation will help you to benefit from the teachers' experience – after all, they know the classes and have been teaching their subject for years.

Discipline
pp 21–3

Classroom management
pp 17–23

Do not fall into the trap of observing the classes as if you were a student. See the class from the teacher's point of view if you want to gain useful tips on how to anticipate problems and deal with them. It is fatal to blame the teachers for any problems that arise instead of watching carefully to see what students are learning and picking up teaching tips and procedures from teachers. It is always useful to imagine yourself being observed. For even the most experienced teacher, an observer can be off-putting. Be clear that you are observing to get to know the students and to find out what you will be expected to do. Note that in some countries, for example Italy, teachers are very rarely observed during their whole teaching career and do not always welcome the idea.

An observation checklist

It helps to make an observation sheet to complete while you are watching classes both to guide you and make a record for each group. Show the teacher what you are doing and get as much information as you can. Keep this observation sheet with a record of the work you cover with the class. This record of your work could be passed on to the next assistant to help give a feel for the school.

Class name .... Teacher ....

Age of students .... Level of English ....

Number of students..

Number of hours per week English studied ....,

Textbook name ....

Type of textbook (traditional, very trendy, colourful) ....

Support materials (readers, dictionaries, extra grammar book)

....

Equipment used (tapes, CD-ROMs, videos, other)

....

Student needs (more structured practice, listening work, tense work, specific exam practice)

....

....

Student difficulties (pronunciation of certain sounds, specific grammar points, reading texts)

....

....

General attitude towards learning English (bored, motivated)

....

....

Classroom management techniques

....

....

How noise level is contained

....

....

How talkative and disruptive pupils are handled

....

....

Modes of working used

* teacher with whole class ....

* pair work ....

* group work ....

* choral repetition ....

* individual work ....

Use of mother tongue

* when? ....

* what for? ....

Classroom language used/familiar to students, (*Open books; Can you ...?*)

....

....

Unit 2 Learning styles and classroom management

The school culture

Each institution, large or small, rural or urban, primary or secondary, has its own culture. This is a set of unwritten rules regarding codes of behaviour: how staff should dress, how they address each other, how teachers and pupils should work together and how discipline problems are dealt with. Find out what these rules are by discreet questioning and observation. Even if you do not agree with them all you must respect the institution which is employing you. Avoid taking matters into your own hands and rely on the advice of colleagues if problems arise. If you behave very differently from the rest of the staff then the students will not know where to place you and will not necessarily respect you as a staff member or teacher of English. Even if you are only employed to assist teachers, remember that in the eyes of the students you are in a teaching role when you take a class alone. The quality of your preparation and how you manage the classes counts most.

Teaching approaches

Approaches to language teaching vary greatly from school to school, not just from country to country. Even if the national directive is to teach languages communicatively, with emphasis on all four skills, in practice this will not necessarily have been taken up at grass roots level. Even within one school one teacher may favour more speaking and listening work, with videos and lots of communication activities, while in the same building a more traditional colleague may prefer to work with more translation and grammar work. Most teachers help themselves to a variety of techniques which they feel comfortable with.

The assistant should bear the following in mind:

- **All teachers have their own style.** Respect their way of working even if you are convinced through reading, training courses or personal experience that other techniques work better for you.

- **It is unwise to rush in and try to change things overnight.** Your role is to facilitate language use but you need to start with the familiar and gradually introduce new ways of working which suit your purpose.

- **Learners from teacher-centred classrooms need to be taught how to collaborate** and work in pairs, etc. and this has to be done gradually to avoid confusion and chaos.

- **The techniques used very much depend on the age range.** Adult learners in a small group in a private language school respond differently from a large group of excited adolescents in a state secondary school. Ball-throwing communication games are great fun in a primary school (although difficult to handle with twenty-five children), but it will not appeal to most adolescents. You have to weigh up the age range factor carefully. Assess the games and activities in ELT books in this light. Most work well with co-operative adults in a UK language school but need real classroom management skills to work in a continental European classroom.

- **Teaching approaches are reflected in the room arrangement.** You may realise that the ideal layout for a classroom is horseshoe-shaped. In a lot of state schools there are fixed, immovable rows of desks with almost no room for the teacher to move between each one. Shifting furniture for group work may be the answer but be wary of noise and the time it takes. Plan ahead and leave the room as you found it.

Management of games
p 93

'I am in two schools and they are so different as to be untrue! In each school I work in a completely different way. Even within the schools the styles I adopt depend on the member of staff I am working with.'
Martin Skitt, Linz, Austria. Assistant in two Gymnasien.

Learning approaches

All learners in institutions are under pressure to achieve similar levels of competence, yet in a large class you will find a varied range of achievement and will have to cater for all (see below). In addition, a naturally chatty teenager will be more likely to be talkative in the language class than his shy friend. Personality is a deciding factor in attitude and competence.

Using diagrams
and time-lines
pp 32–4

Learner attitudes
to role playing
p 44

Dictogloss
p 84

Mind maps
p 78

Some people learn better from seeing things, and enjoy diagrams, writing things down and reading. Other people have an instinctive ear and like learning from hearing and listening, while others prefer action such as making things with their hands, and walking about.

Most of us are a mixture. Clearly lessons which focus solely on the written word with little visual support disadvantage some learners. We need to give a variety of tasks that help students learn in different ways. Accept that during an hour-long lesson the learners' interest will wane at some point if the activity in hand doesn't appeal to their way of working. It is impossible to please everybody all the time but we can try and stimulate as many as possible in the hour we have. This means it is unwise to spend a whole hour on one activity. Some learners will instinctively take to role play even if their command of English makes it challenging. Others may dislike role play, putting on a show, exposing themselves publicly or *pretending*. Be aware and plan for these learning preferences.

Handling role play
pp 44–5

Think about your own preferred learning style:

- What sort of language activities did you enjoy most at school?

- How do you learn new words?

- Are you better at writing or speaking your languages? Have you got an ear for accents?

- Do you like to work alone, in a pair or in a large group?

- Do you need to take notes? Do you like making tables and diagrams to help you study?

Establishing a rapport with your students

The first time in front of a class by yourself can be nerve-wracking. They may well know that you are not a qualified teacher and, particularly with adolescents, you will have to earn their trust and respect. Your main wish might be to be friendly and liked by these students but this will come with time. First you need to establish yourself as the leader of the class. Once you have control of the group and they are working well together with you and each other then there will be time for jokes and friendly banter. This is particularly important with large groups of teenagers who are excited to have a new face but also ready to trip you up if you seem unsure.

Motivating activities for teenagers
pp 99–101

Teacher talking time
p 36

- **Appear confident**. If you are very nervous it will bother them and some will take advantage. Remember the trainee teachers you had at secondary school?

- **Establish a professional and not a personal relationship**. Be welcoming and make a real effort to learn their names and use them. Make a seating plan and get them to make name cards for their desks if this helps you.

- **Be well prepared**. Set the agenda and have a plan which you all follow. Don't ask them what they would like to do or what they want to talk about. They need to see you as responsible and reliable. Later in the year with older learners there may be times when you can choose discussion topics together, but not in the initial stages.

- **Impose your presence**. This does not mean that you take centre stage and do all the talking. Your speaking style (clear and loud enough for all) and your physical presence in a large class help to manage the room. Avoid sitting behind a desk or standing in a corner. Move around, interact with all pupils at the questioning stages, scan the room and make eye contact as if in the theatre. Looking as if you are the teacher reassures learners, and being lively will show that you are enthusiastic about teaching and learning.

The assistant as speech model
p 57

- **Listen to the students**. Show interest and listen to their replies to your questions. Be patient if they take time to reply. Wait a bit longer for students to reply as they need to get used to your voice and think about your questions.

- **Pay attention to your own voice and speech**. Modify your speed without distorting sounds or putting in artificial pauses mid-sentence. Pause after each sentence a bit longer than you would for a native speaker.

One disadvantage of working with adolescents is that they are not always enthusiastic when you suggest an activity, but once they get involved in it any objections disappear.

'At first I was very put off by my pupils whingeing when I told them what we were going to do. You have to expect this! Basically, don't take anything personally. Get them on your side and you'll all have fun'. **Susan Young, Loire region, France. Assistant in a secondary and a primary school.**

Getting students used to an English-only classroom

Motivating learners
to use English
pp 25–6

After observation, you may note that a good deal of the mother tongue is used during the lesson or that some is used for instructions. Talk this over with teachers if it becomes an issue, but it is advisable for you to start in English and continue. For classes unused to an English-only environment you will need to teach classroom language through gesture, mime, flashcards or a chart. This will take time, especially with beginners. Simple instructions like *'listen', 'open your books', 'ask your partner'*, etc. can be gradually built up over the first few days. Make your own comments as simple and as natural as possible: *'Really?', 'That's a good idea Sylvie', 'What do you think Lorenzo?', 'I enjoyed your dialogues. Now let's look at ...', 'Who's next?'* Try to establish a limited but realistic range for all groups to cope with. They will soon start imitating you.

Eliciting from visuals,
key words and
headlines
p 50

Ideas for the first lessons alone with the class

You can plan your first lessons (see suggestions below) before you arrive, as many activities can be adapted depending on the level of students. These are open-ended activities which generate language at all levels. They will also help you see how much language the classes can use. Your expectations in terms of question types will differ from controlled beginner level. For example, from *'Is that your brother/boyfriend?' 'Is that your home town?'* to far more complex questioning for intermediate teenage learners. Give students headings as prompts to the topic area they are asking about, e.g. home life, family life, spare time.

Photographs

Personalising tasks
p 52

Take a collection of personal photos (your family, your friends, your home town, your university town, pets, etc.) and encourage the students to ask you about the pictures. Build questions on the board and ask students about themselves using the same questions. This is also a quick way to gauge their level of English. It can be followed up with photos or pictures of students' families and backgrounds in the next lesson.

What's in your school bag?

Take out of your bag a series of objects and explain each object one by one. Students can ask questions. You can prompt answers and involvement from them. *'Have you got a book in your bag Louis?' 'What's the title?' 'Do you like maths?' 'Is maths your favourite subject?'*

Examples:

'This is my lucky key ring. I bought it on holiday.' 'Where did you go?' 'Where is it from?'

'I've got a picture of my favourite pop star here and this is a magazine I like reading.'

'Who is your favourite pop star?' 'Do you like reading?' 'What do you like reading?'

Personalising games
p 94

Classroom management (groups and large classes)

Changes of pace

All of the best laid plans can go wrong. Perhaps the students find the text you chose unexpectedly difficult. You planned a listening task but the cassette recorder won't work. Students are losing interest and the amount of chattering is increasing. Students have enjoyed the game so much that they have become over-excited and need calming down. This calls for a change of pace, a slower more reflective activity or a livelier task.

You will also need to add variety to your weekly lesson routine or you and the pupils will lose interest.

'I found it really good to vary the lessons – one week text, one week a game, one week a song and text work, etc.' **Vanessa Garfield, Valence, France. Assistant in a collège and a lycée.**

Dealing with the unexpected

- Abandon something that isn't really working rather than flog a dead horse, but have a filler activity to use as back-up.

- Always have a contingency plan if you are relying on equipment that might go wrong.

- Keep some fillers in your bag which correspond to the month's work. These can be ten-minute activities which liven up a dull, uninterested room (usually speaking/listening game or contest) or calm down an unruly lot (usually reading or writing based).

- Collect a battery of multi-purpose texts for use in emergencies.

- Keep a small collection of large detailed pictures and/or photos on a theme or topic related to the term's work. You can cut a collection of photos from newspapers (even local foreign ones) and magazine supplements to use with higher levels. Update and check photos regularly. For example:

  – give out two or three photos to small groups or pairs or whole class

  – students write words associated with the person or event

  – students invent a headline or match a headline you give on the board to the photo

  – students prepare short oral description of photo – what it shows, which event it represents, etc.

Case study: 'Drilling drowned out my lesson plan'

An assistant who had a perfectly usable video recorder found that there was so much building work and drilling going on outside that students couldn't hear. Thinking on her feet, without any back-up plans, she decided to generate language anyway. She used the video as a silent movie for brainstorming vocabulary. Then in pairs students watched the video again and tried to retell the story with the vocabulary written on the board. Finally, they looked at one or two small exchanges of dialogue with no sound and imagined what the speakers were saying, then acted out their dialogues. A full lesson with no sound.

'Something which has helped me and saved my skin several times has been to have three or four varied lessons prepared in my bag at all times … you never know when a teacher will suddenly say "Oh, can you do next lesson instead of the eight o'clock on Monday" – and you really want to be able to say "Yes" to that!' **Richard Hewitt, Eisenstadt, Austria. Assistant in a secondary school and Further Education college.**

'Be flexible. If the teacher gives you some material with one class, exploit it and use it with others.' **Alexis Hughes, Chambéry, France. Assistant in a lycée.**

Dealing with large classes of mixed ability

Mixed classes usually comprise students who have arrived at varying levels of achievement. This does not mean that the weakest at speaking are not as capable at language learning. Some may have had no English at primary school while others may have had three years. In a secondary school some may be very good at reading a poem and understanding it, but not accustomed to discussing the meaning in English and lack the vocabulary to do so.

Difficulties	Solutions
Producing tasks which all students can complete.	Use mainly open-ended tasks where learners brainstorm and contribute what they know.
Some able students finish first and get bored and disruptive.	Give tasks which have a core part that everyone has to finish and optional extra questions too.
There is a wide range of levels and you risk teaching three different lessons.	Try mainly collaborative tasks with small groups of mixed ability so they help each other and pool ideas/skills.
Some need revision and the others don't.	Make revision into a team/pair game.
Some texts and listenings are too easy for some.	Choose content/topics very interesting for the age range so the ideas hold their interest.

Student-generated revision
pp 99–100

Building resources
pp 126–37

Pooling task types
pp 31, 41, 43, 72, 78, 84, 100

Revision games
pp 99–101

Getting the listening level right
pp 81–83

19

Setting up a pair work system

Always follow a similar procedure so that once it is familiar, students will respond automatically and know what is expected.

Pair work for lower levels pp 37–41

- **Assign roles clearly around the class**, pointing to each student in turn. *'You are A … you are B …, etc.'* or use colours, animals, etc. with younger learners.

- **Double-check they know their role** with a show of hands. *'Hands up As … hands up Bs'* or *'Who's red?' 'Who's a tiger?'*

- **Don't explain what they have to do, demonstrate**. Take one student, he is A and you are B. Practise the dialogue/exchange. Double-check with one pair of students who play A and B and act out with you prompting the pair work. Put prompts on the board if this helps lower levels or classes unsure about pair work.

Prompts on board	student A	'… from?'
	student B	'I'm …'

- **Use choral repetition to reinforce roles if necessary**. All As say their lines in chorus. Pick on a student B to respond. Repeat with Bs.

Management of games p 93

- **Only let students start when you are sure they are all clear as to what they are supposed to be doing**. Use this technique for all communication games and it will get faster and more efficient as they get used to working without you. Never try to set up pair work without checking that the instructions are clear. Think how you will set it up before the lesson.

- **Quickly circulate when they start** in order to see if each of the pairs is clear and working together. Help individual pairs with prompting. Keep an eye out for waning interest and don't let it go on too long. Are they near to exchanging all the information they needed to exchange? Be ready to call a halt.

- **Change pairs with the minimum of fuss and noise** as this can be a big time-waster in large classes and annoy colleagues in nearby classrooms. Try not to say *'Find a new partner …'* as the whole room could be set in motion. All students turn round quietly and form a pair with someone behind or in front or on the other side. Make all As stand up (no scraping chairs) and on the count of three move two desks down, up or across to find a new partner.

Finishing off

Many assistants find it difficult to judge how long activities will take and find themselves either running out of time or with fifteen more minutes to go and nothing to do. This is true for all teachers, but it improves as you get to know your classes. However, plan ahead and start winding down well before the bell rings so you can give a summary of the lesson. After a discussion or simple oral task you may need to go over main problems on the board and must allow time for this essential feedback. In some schools pupils just pack up and rush off when the bell rings. Try to avoid this. Insist on a formal conclusion and goodbye. If you are required to give homework or to ask students to prepare a task such as something for the role play in the next lesson, do not do it at the very end. Attention usually wanes by the end, so give forewarning and instructions earlier and then just a final reminder at the end.

Student summaries
pp 53–4

Discipline problems and solutions

Factors leading to discipline problems

- a gap in the lesson (bad planning, an activity loses momentum, a piece of equipment fails to work)

- unclear instructions (they don't know what to do, they don't start and attention wanders)

- overexcited students arrive from another class in a rowdy mood

- lack of teacher attention (you need constantly to scan the room and keep your eyes and ears open to what is happening, especially in large groups)

- the assistant concentrates on lengthy explanations to one individual (the others get bored)

Correcting students
pp 28–31

- work is too easy or too challenging (students give up or attention wanders).

Always discuss discipline procedures with members of staff in your host school before you start teaching. Each country has different rules and expectations and this can vary from school to school. One assistant commented wryly that the discipline methods used on him at school would get you the sack in his host country. In some teaching cultures a quiet classroom is considered a disciplined classroom where learning is taking place. This is evidently at odds with your role

The school culture
p 12

which is to maximise student talking opportunities, with reasonable noise levels! Clearly a class that is in control is not always quiet and a quiet class with a teacher doing all the talking is not necessarily a good learning environment. You will create healthy chatter in oral classes but this must not descend into anarchy! However, bear in mind that teachers on either side of your classroom might take a different view if your class noise disturbs their lessons. Try not to assume that the teacher you are working with is traditional or boring because they do not use the riotous communication games their students adore doing with you. It could be that these teachers have met with criticism or opposition from colleagues in the past due to noise generated from their language classrooms!

Typical problems and some suggested approaches

- **One student starts talking to another and keeps on doing it**. Ask one of the students a question as soon as you realise they are becoming disruptive. Move nearer to them as you move around the room and try to make eye contact. If eye contact and interruption are not sufficient then move the students to different seats.

- **Students are all talking and no one is listening**. Try to establish silence without raising your voice. Clap loudly, tap a ruler on the board, count down from ten (some students will join in chorus). When silence is reached … hold the silence for a minute or so before resuming. If disruption is due to lack of interest in the task, go on to something else (a filler) to change pace.

- **A student deliberately refuses to do an activity you have prepared**. Assign a different role if it is an oral task, e.g. this student records the dialogue on a tape or becomes the group secretary in a discussion by writing notes on what is said. Explain that any work not completed in class must be done at home as homework. If it continues, see if the student can be removed from the group for your lessons.

- **A student starts shouting at you**. It is difficult not to shout back or lose your cool but try to remain calm and firm. Wait for the student to calm down but if this fails and the situation escalates, call for assistance or send another student for assistance. Try to resolve the situation by assigning a task to the rest of the class and taking the angry student aside for a quiet word.

Be wary of the following techniques which might not be used or allowed in classrooms and which are not always effective:

- threats

- giving lines

- public humiliation by putting them in the corner

- giving written homework

- putting them in the corridor (they could leave the premises!)

- shouting loudly

- punishing the whole class for the behaviour of a few.

Unit 3 Motivation and progress

Factors influencing learner motivation

- **The status of English**. Its perceived usefulness in school and after school.

- **Past learning experience**. Students moving to one institution from another where there may have been a negative approach to English need to regain interest and faith in their ability to learn it.

- **Success and reward**. If students have successfully completed previous tasks and lessons and been praised for their achievement then they are more inclined to make an effort.

- **The content of the lesson**. This must be inherently of interest to the age range. They need to be able to identify with the topics chosen.

- **Self-confidence**. Some learners are very disheartened by little failures and some are very nervous about making mistakes, so hindering their progress.

- **Length of time studying English**. At the early stages of language learning everything is new and progress can seem rapid. This sense of achievement is lost or gets slower as the years pass. This is one of the reasons why children at primary school or in their first years of English at lower secondary seem so much more motivated than adolescents in upper secondary school.

- **Lack of challenge**. To get a sense of progress and to create the feelings of effort that students associate with learning, we need to stretch them, e.g. don't tell learners something they can tell you, given a little guidance and encouragement. Help them to guess new words instead of jumping in with translations, or encourage them to try to correct their own mistakes on the basis of their knowledge.

- **A sense of difficulty**. We can create a feeling that English is a difficult language without realising it, with chance remarks like *'there are lots of irregulars in English'* or *'this isn't as simple as your language'*. It is common to hear students say of their own language *'Italian is very difficult', 'French grammar is very complicated'*. More often than not these negative feelings have been induced by learning approaches which over-emphasised difficulties and over-highlighted learners' errors. Such comparisons are fruitless and undermine confidence.

Different learning approaches pp 13–14

We cannot take for granted that learners studying English in a compulsory school system will be motivated in the way that a young adult, paying lots of money, in a private language school of his choice will be. You too have chosen to study languages and perceive it as useful (although research in the EU has shown that you would be in a distinct minority in the UK). English may be perceived as the most important language to learn in school systems abroad and by parents, but this perception is not necessarily taken on board by students. English is just another school subject. Misunderstandings and disappointment occur when the assistant uses an applauded technique or task from a seminar on teaching motivated young adults, or from an ELT book developed mainly through experimentation in private language schools. Too often the comments on quite normal adolescents become negative: *'they don't care'* or *'they are lazy'* or *'they don't make an effort'*. However, it could be that the approach wasn't suitable for teenagers or was just too far removed from their usual learning experience. You certainly need a great deal of classroom management skills to cope with the demands of a large class of fourteen-year-olds compared to a small group of co-operative twenty-five-year-olds on holiday in Oxford. It pays not to be too harsh on yourself or on the learners. Try not to be too quick to blame yourself or them. Accepting your limitations, and theirs, will help you plan for a more appropriate lesson next time.

The needs of
adolescents
in a culture lesson
pp 110–12

Using English in the classroom

Some of your students will not be used to an English-only classroom. It is advisable for them to make the most of your mother-tongue status but it can sometimes be difficult to insist on English-only. In some school systems translation is used, particularly in a contrastive way, to highlight differences between the native language tense system or use of prepositions, etc. and the relative usage in English. These uses can be constructive but assistants are generally not called upon to present language, just to reinforce and practise it. Therefore your lessons should be in English, except in exceptional circumstances, like a student falling ill or major misunderstanding that can only be cleared up in the native language.

Providing a good
model
of spoken English
pp 56–7

Tips for encouraging the use of English in the classroom

- **Always reply in English**, even if students are speaking in their own language.

- **Try not to be too dogmatic**, but comments like *'It's easier for me to speak English – and it helps you'* can explain your approach.

- **Artificial motivators** like the swear box for use of the students' mother tongue can be introduced in a light-hearted way, or a list of forfeits which anyone not speaking in English must carry out. Use dice and a list of six forfeits (which you can vary throughout the year), e.g. *'Count from twenty backwards very quickly'*, *'Sing a song you know in English'*, etc.

- **Points can be deducted** from the team score during games or contests if the mother tongue is used.

- **Make it clear** to the students that you do not welcome the use of the mother tongue in your classes. If this proves to be a problem, report it to the teacher in charge.

Classroom English
p 16

- **Simplify the English you use** to suit the comprehension level of the class and stick to a clear body of classroom instructions which are concise and supported by gesture if appropriate. This does not mean speaking in monosyllables or broken English. Use tone of voice, stress, intonation and any visual methods to aid understanding.

Visual aids
pp 68–79

- **Help students to make an effort to understand** without depending on a quick translation. This can take time in groups not used to making intelligent guesses or deducing meaning from context.

Types of learner error

It is useful for you and the learners to accept that mistakes are an inevitable and natural part of the learning process. It is through learners' mistakes that we can see what they are struggling to master, what concepts they have misunderstood and what extra work they might need.

Interference from the mother tongue

All languages are different and it is natural to assume that other languages might perform in the same way as our own. Our system of reality, which defines how we view the world, often collapses when we try to apply it to another. In European languages there may be two forms to denote the *'you'* of English and these forms are used depending on how well you know someone in your own social hierarchy, such as using *vous* or *tu* in French and *Lei* or *tu* in Italian.

When a French or Italian learner says: *'I am living in Nice with my parents'*, rather than *'I live in ...'*, it is because their own language does not have two present tense forms to distinguish between permanent/fixed time and continuous/temporary fixed time. It is common for learners to ask *'What is the future tense in English?'* as if looking for a direct translation. These assumptions show up in their errors and are natural.

Translation

Sometimes when speaking or writing, students may find they do not know a suitable expression, so they fall back on using a direct translation of their own language. This is a conscious decision, rather than the unconscious interference. For example, a German speaker might say *'it makes me nothing out'* instead of *'I don't mind'*. It is useful to develop communication strategies to get the message across, and this is more successful in the long term than staying silent. Experimentation is a vital part of the process towards fluency.

False friends

Some words may have been borrowed from other European languages, notably Latin in origin, and look the same as a word in your own language. This 'false' assumption leads us to think they mean the same and can be used in the same way: e.g. *Embarazada* = 'pregnant' in Spanish, and not the English *embarrassed*. *Attualmente* = 'at the moment' in Italian, and not the English *actually*.

Sound system

Each language has its own sounds, which are produced by using the throat, mouth, tongue, etc. This involves basic motor skills, which differ from one language to another and need time and effort to master. (See Unit 6 Speech work).

Cultural competence
p 105

Getting your message across
p 68

Question practice for developing fluency
pp 96–7

Pronunciation practice
pp 60–5

Basic pronunciation table
p 130

27

When and how to correct errors

Fluency versus accuracy

Controlled oral practice
pp 37–41

When giving tasks to learners we need to make it clear if we are focusing on accuracy or fluency. It is important to learn to use language correctly as too many mistakes will impede understanding. However, we also need to get our message across with reasonable speed and choice of appropriate content that suits our message. When this fluency is missing, you have a very correct, laboured and robot-like delivery. All this does not mean giving them a lecture on language learning. Simply indicate with a comment: *'I will not correct you during these dialogues because I want you to try to speak as naturally as possible'*, or *'Be careful to use the words "do" or "does" when asking your questions'*.

The school culture
p 12

When to correct?

Observing classes
pp 9–11

It is generally best not to interrupt students in mid-speech during fluency work. However, intervene with help if communication breaks down. If the learner has got most of his work right but has made a trivial mistake, it is sometimes wise to let the mistake pass. We can sometimes be over-keen for them to get everything right, but this can mean that they then feel over-corrected without getting encouragement for the little that they have managed to achieve. Conversely some assistants don't want to be too harsh, and regularly fail to pick up on mistakes which need attention, for fear of discouraging the learners. In a school setting learners are accustomed on a daily basis to getting things 'right' or 'wrong' and may be less sensitive than you think. Observe their teachers. How do they correct? When? Have they a policy regarding accuracy or fluency work? Weigh all this up before deciding what is best for you and the learners.

Correction techniques

The assistant as visual aid
p 68

Some students do not want you to correct every single error as this is demotivating. A study of fourteen- to fifteen-year-olds in Italian secondary schools showed that they cannot absorb more than a certain amount of corrective feedback. Written work covered in red pen can be disheartening too. However, if learners are not aware that they have made an error then they cannot remedy it. We therefore need to use a variety of techniques to help them spot areas of difficulty.

Feedback on errors

Learners expect and need feedback, and so do teachers, and this can take a number of forms:

Verbal praise or encouragement in class

Be aware that during your lessons students need encouraging words when they have answered well or completed a task. The danger is to over-praise and devalue the effect by constantly gushing *'very good'*. Encourage with nods, smiles and *'right, fine'*, but keep extra special praise for specific moments.

Discussing progress with teachers

The assistant should not be expected to assess students, although some teachers expect this and the matter should be discussed tactfully. It is only natural for the teacher to want to know how learners are doing with you, especially if you are left alone with them. Try to keep this feedback to a monthly or termly session to discuss general details, but keep your own records of how students are doing, what has improved and what the common problems are.

Written praise of their written work

Learners may demand a mark and be very dependent on the marking systems in their schools. Try to avoid this, but use comments like: *'Very good. I like your ideas'.* With younger learners use symbols, such as a smiley face with details added for extra good work, like a smiley face with a top hat and bow tie. If the work is fair but there are quite a few errors, do a face which is half happy, half sad. If something is good or poor, try to give a sentence which explains why.

Recording students

Record students' conversations or role plays and use this for your own analysis and even for students' self-assessment. It can be good for motivation if students have a recording of themselves at the beginning of a year, so they can hear how much their performance has improved at the end of the year. Select only very short extracts for students to hear.

Relations with
teachers
pp 3–8

Visual correction techniques

Use hand gestures for clarification and for encouraging self-correction:

- **Use your index finger and thumb to indicate contractions**. When a student speaks in the full form, raise your arm and bring your index finger and thumb together which signals that a contraction was necessary. Students quickly get used to this and self-correct.

  Example: 'I would like to go to ...' (teacher signals) ... 'Oh, ... I'd like to go to the cinema this weekend.' See figure one.

- **Use all the fingers on one hand to represent the words in a sentence or question**. If there is a missing auxiliary, wiggle the finger where it is missing, leaving a silent gap as you say the sentence.

  Example: *'Where you going tomorrow?'* (Teacher repeats the learner's question indicating each finger to represent the words, including a finger for the missing item, *'are'*.) Student then self-corrects: *'Where ... are ... you going tomorrow?'* (Teacher praises correction.)

  Your fingers can also indicate visually where a problem lies.

  Example: Student: 'I haven't finished my homework already.' (Teacher repeats phrase with a questioning tone, wiggling finger to represent already.) Student: 'Already?' (Teacher nods.) 'Oh, yes ... I haven't finished my homework yet.' (Teacher praises.) See figure two.

- **Use your arm or hand to gesture for inversion in question forms**.

  Example: Student: 'Where you have been?' (Teacher crosses over hands in a sweeping movement.) Student: "Where ... been ... no ... Where have you been?' (Teacher nods, praises self-correction.) See figure three.

Fig. 1	Fig. 2	Fig. 3
Contractions	**Indicating where error lies**	**Inversion**

Correction during fluency activities

We tend to intervene more during accuracy work. In this case it would be appropriate to use any of the methods above. However, if you do not want to interrupt the general flow in conversation during a fluency task, it is best to keep a mental note to follow up later. However, you can correct more unobtrusively in a similar way to that used by a mother correcting her own child learning to speak: Child: *'We goed to the park with Gran.'* Mother: *'Yes, we went to the park with her and it was lovely, wasn't it?'* You don't highlight the source of the error but you give confirmation of the correct model. It feels less severe to students who need to be corrected during fluency activities.

Fluency tasks
pp 41–5, 97–8

Encouraging peer or self-correction

- When correcting written work put a line to indicate where the error is, but don't correct it. It helps if you indicate in the margin what type of error it is with symbols, e.g. *w/o* for word order, sp for spelling, etc. *'My father like__ football but I don't!'* (Third person?) The learners then have to puzzle over their errors, discuss with classmates and, if necessary, the teacher, to come up with a solution.

- You can use the same approach as above during oral feedback on the board. Select the main error types. Write four or five on the board with an indication of where the problem lies. Put students in pairs for a few minutes to correct the problems. This might be pronunciation, but with higher level groups you can also focus on appropriate context, e.g. *'Was the expression polite enough?'* *'Was it too formal?'*

Making revision fun
pp 99–101

- Activities involving group writing will naturally involve a certain amount of peer correction as students contribute their knowledge to the group effort. To take this a step further, students can be encouraged to pass round their group work to be marked by another group before handing it in. This can be very motivating for teenagers who value the opinion of their peers.

Visual aids
pp 68–79

- To reinforce feelings of progress get students to collect their most frequent errors weekly. Students copy the uncorrected phrase, question or word on a piece of card or paper and keep in an envelope or small box. Put a corrected version in another envelope or box. Encourage them to look at the uncorrected version frequently for five minutes every day. When they are sure that they are not making the mistake any more, they remove the uncorrected version from their envelope and transfer it to the envelope with the corrected version to form a pair. Students may also like swapping error envelopes in class once a month and then try to correct them orally or in writing. This gives teenagers a sense of control over their own progress.

Clarification techniques to use during feedback

Diagrams

Diagrams are particularly useful in representing abstract concepts of time, quantity and degree. You can use them:

- to clarify confusion

- to give a board summary which students can refer to

- as prompts on the board for learners to use during controlled oral work or discussions.

Card games
pp 95–6

Some diagrams can be used to illustrate a variety of concepts (see below), but don't overuse them if you want them to associate the pictures with a main concept. If they are popular you can make small versions in packs to give to pairs or small groups who use them as a card game.

Diagrams for degree. Draw on board or take five sheets of A4 paper and black marker. Stick each on to card and laminate or cover with self-adhesive plastic film so they can be re-used. Write the various uses on the back as they come up in your teaching.

'Do you ever see films in English on television?'
'Yes, sometimes.' / 'No, never.'

Fig. 4 **Diagrams showing degree**

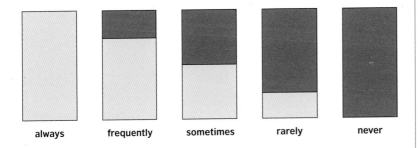

| always | frequently | sometimes | rarely | never |

You can use the same sequence of diagrams in many ways:

Example: *'What do you think of Rap?'*

Love / Like a lot / Quite like / Don't like ... much / Don't like ... at all

Use only two or three of the visuals as prompts then use the others to complete students' understanding of shades of meaning.

Example: *'I think that all schools should ban make-up.' 'Well, I agree in part but don't you think that ...?'*

Completely agree / Agree in part / Completely disagree

Then you can explore: *'I hardly agree ...'*

Time-lines

These are very useful for:

- *contrasting tenses (past/present)*
  He was an English teacher but now he's an international pop star.

- *contrasting a period with a fixed point in time (future and past)*
  It was raining when we arrived at Kate's flat.

- *contrasting continuous with interrupted actions*
  He left the village that night and has lived in London ever since.

Fig. 5 **Example of a time-line**

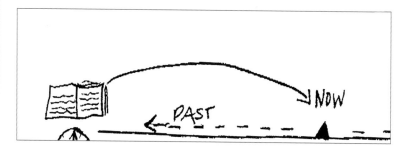

These diagrammatic forms genuinely help students. French, Spanish and Italian learners can be helped with understanding perfect tense forms using these time-lines. Students starting with time-lines need to understand the first concept that the point on the line marked **now** refers to the moment that the speaker is speaking.

You can use the time-lines to elicit questions or answers in preparation for a task, as a way to clear up problems during feedback after oral work and as a concept check to see if they understand the use of tenses. Ask a student or students to complete a board time-line in their notebooks to illustrate the sentence.

Example: *I have been living in Rouen since July 2001 and I lived in Paris from 1990 until July 2001.*

Unit 4 Oral practice

Fluency
versus accuracy
p 28

Using the
learner's world
pp 52, 94, 110

Information
gap activities
pp 40, 75–6

Conversational
strategies
pp 46–55

Setting up
pair work
p 20

What do speaking skills involve?

Speaking a language involves using the components correctly – making the right sounds, choosing the right words and getting constructions grammatically correct. Pronunciation, grammar and vocabulary tasks will focus on the need for practice in language accuracy. At the same time, we also need to get a clear message across and this involves choosing appropriate content or ideas to suit a situation, e.g. deciding what is polite or what might appear rude, how to interrupt or how to participate in a conversation. All this involves practice in language fluency. Both types of practice are equally important, although some traditional approaches can concentrate rather too much on accuracy tasks which result in students speaking like a grammar book.

How to prepare students for real communication in English

- **Personal response**. Give students tasks which ask them to contribute information about themselves.

- **Variety of responses**. Give them dialogues which require more than one set response so they have to decide and create their own dialogues.

- **Work in pairs or groups**. Give students tasks in which they have to communicate with others to exchange information, as this gives a greater number of students a chance to talk.

- **Varied language**. Give tasks which require the use of more than one type of sentence structure so students get practice in combining different language forms, e.g. tenses.

- **Balance accuracy tasks with fluency work**. Make it clear that you are interested in what students are saying, not just how grammatically correct they are being! Encourage them to show verbal signs of interest: *'Really? That's interesting, I didn't know that!', 'I think that's a good idea!', 'Are you?', 'Did you?'*.

- **Less teacher talking time**. Be careful not to do all the talking, and aim for student participation from the very start of lessons. When preparing pair work, bring in student responses, use students to rehearse roles, get all the class to repeat key items and try to avoid lengthy explanations. Demonstrate. Keep your own talking to a minimum during the activities.

Controlled speaking activities

To understand the degree of control in a speaking task we can contrast these two diary activities:

Diary activity task A

Fig. 1

	Student A
M	visit grandma 3pm painting class 7pm
T	swimming lesson 2–4pm
W	Spanish class 7pm
T	football practice 7pm
F	piano lesson 5pm

	Student B
M	tennis lesson 3pm mum's birthday party pm
T	pub party 6pm
W	Dentist 3pm
T	English club 3pm
F	play rehearsal 6.30pm

Telephone your partner to organise a night out at the cinema or a game of tennis. Find a time which suits both of you. Ask and answer like this:

'What are you doing on Monday evening/afternoon?'
'Are you doing anything on Tuesday/Wednesday afternoon?'

'I'm not free. I'm going to my painting class.'
'Yes, I am. I'm going to school/to the dentist.'

Diary activity task B

Fig. 2

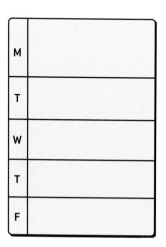

M	
T	
W	
T	
F	

> Complete this diary with six appointments or activities over the whole week. Phone your friend to organise an evening out (you suggest the activity) or an afternoon together. Try and fix one fun activity together.

Task A is far more controlled:

- the language structures to use are indicated
- the diary pages contain all the necessary vocabulary for making appointments
- the content is determined by the teacher.

Task B is far less controlled and linguistically more demanding:

- students choose the language to use
- students put in the content and make decisions about their intentions.

Card games
pp 95–6

It would be possible to modify each task depending on the levels of your classes and their need for fluency or accuracy work. The amount of linguistic support and ideas you give will determine the level of difficulty of the task.

Board or picture prompts for dialogue practice

Dialogue-building gives students with little English a chance to practise beyond sentence level. Making these dialogues meaningful is essential for interest and motivation. Our approach to building the dialogues might involve giving students prompts on cards or on the board. Contrast the two different types of prompting below:

1 **A mechanical drill from a traditional textbook**

Students find these very boring.

> *'You are a stranger in your town and you need directions. Make up your questions:'*
>
> Music shop. *('Is there a music shop near here?')*
>
> a) swimming pool   b) disco   c) café   d) tourist office   e) cinema

You can make these questions without even thinking about it. The nonsensical prompt *thingy* would still produce the accurate question:
'Is there a thingy near here?'.

2 **A meaningful dialogue**

Students must understand the situation in order to respond and must think about what to say. This is naturally more demanding but ultimately more beneficial for learning.

> *'You are a stranger in your town and you need some things.*
> *Ask directions to the places.'*
>
> You need a map. *('Is there a tourist office near here?')*
>
> a) some toothpaste   b) to change some traveller's cheques
> c) something to drink d) some stamps

Factors influencing learner motivation pp 24–5

Information gap

Spot the difference
pp 75–6

Traditional approaches often require students to reproduce a written dialogue verbally. This does not prepare them for the unpredictable nature of real communication where the person you are speaking to has information you do not know. Information gap is less artificial, providing a purpose to speak since the other person possesses some information that you need to know.

For example, one student has an incomplete set of instructions on how to get to a friend's party and is not sure what time it starts. The other student has been to the house before and has a map of how to get there. He also has an invitation which states the time. They phone each other to get details.

Visual aids
pp 68–79

In the above example, if both students had the same handout the conversation would be artificial and pointless. Why tell each other details that they both know anyway? However, the information gap forces them to arrive at a complete set of facts after exchanging the missing parts. Through tables of facts that are incomplete, maps which have places missing, drawings with missing parts, timetables, brochures and many more visual props, you can simulate real communication gaps for controlled practice work.

Information gap task

Student A – you live in Brighton
Your friend from London has invited you to a concert at Wembley.
He wants to meet you at Waterloo station at around 5 or 6 o'clock so you can travel together to the concert. Ring the station to find a suitable train from Brighton to Waterloo. Find out how much it will cost.

Student B – you work in Brighton station
Use your timetable to answer Student A's questions. Find a suitable train for him/her. Use the price guide to calculate the cost of the ticket.

Activities for controlled practice at all levels

- **Find someone who ...** (activities which focus on specific structures and involve the whole class)

  Example: *'Find someone in this class who can: play a musical instrument; speak another language; dance; cook an Italian meal; play chess; say the alphabet backwards in English; drive a car.'*

- **Questionnaires** (like those in teen magazines)

  Example: *'Are you adventurous or over-cautious?'*
  What would you do if: a) ...?   b) ...?   c) ...?'

You can focus on a structure and vocabulary area. Students have a plan to follow. They complete the questionnaire for their partner then do the scoring. This is a very controlled way of giving speaking practice and it appeals to teenagers.

Using questionnaires for discussion
p 50

Types of fluency practice

If students are more used to teacher-controlled activities and tasks which focus on accuracy, they will need time to get used to fluency activities. Fluency activities are essential at all levels but the balance between fluency and accuracy tasks will differ. You will be able to do far more free activities with intermediate students and upwards, whereas there will be more need for supported and controlled work with absolute beginners and false beginners.

Adapting listening up or down a level
pp 82–3

Tips for fluency practice

- **Base the tasks on language that is lower** than the language used in intensive study (e.g. reading texts) with the class. Learners should be able to find the words they need easily rather than struggle, as this will hinder their chances of speaking fluently. Focus on language areas that they can recall and use well. If they have just been presented with the second conditional you cannot expect them to be using it fluently, although you can have a controlled activity for extra practice in using it.

Error correction techniques
pp 28–32

Correction during
fluency activities
p 31

- **For higher levels, give practice in speaking at length**, not just short exchanges as part of a debate. This means tasks like telling a story or anecdote, telling jokes, making speeches, telling the plot of a book or film or describing a person or place in detail.

- **Keep your intervention to a minimum** while students are performing the task.

- **Prepare vocabulary and ideas** well with students before starting. Students accustomed to more teacher control and to tasks which focus on little more than the repetition of sentences may panic and feel abandoned at first. The first signs of this are a (seemingly) uninterested or downright hostile group of students! They may be in a school culture where the teacher should be seen to be teaching in order for them to feel they are learning! This can happen even after they have enjoyed and successfully completed a task. The key words are **patience** and **preparation**.

Examples of fluency tasks:

- **Talking about yourself.** E.g. *'I hate maths, do you?'*

> Look at this list of subjects we study at school: English; history; maths; art; information technology; geography; physics; chemistry; literature; biology; physical education; design; music.
>
> Choose one subject you like and think of three reasons why you like it. Choose one subject you don't like and think of three reasons why you dislike it.
>
> Ask your partner/group/class about their subjects. Does anyone like the same one as you? Have they got similar reasons? Find out their reasons and make notes under the following headings:

- **Reasons for liking a subject. Reasons for disliking a subject**
  (Adapted from an exercise by Rob Nolasco)

  Prepare the task by using your school timetable, and encourage students to ask you why you liked a subject. This helps vocabulary brainstorming, and you can tailor this to suit the needs of your group. With higher level groups this can lead into a discussion on the ways of studying they prefer, what they might study or do after school, how to make a subject interesting, etc.

- **Giving your opinion**. The easiest way to elicit opinions is to give a list of opinions on a subject or issue and ask students to modify the statements in pairs or groups to reflect their general feelings about the issue. Five or six statements are enough for students to work with. For example, suitable topics could be pocket/spending money and young people working; single-sex or mixed schooling; homework or no homework after school; free use of the Internet at home or restricted parental control of its use.

- **Group planning tasks**. Give a group of students a problem to solve or a list of activities to plan. Coming to an agreement can generate a lot of language.

  Example: '*A group of English students are coming to your town/school next Easter. Prepare a mini booklet to help them. Give a short list of essentials that you think they might need for a three-week stay and give them some useful background information on school life and social life so they are prepared for their arrival.*'

- **Retelling a story or piecing together a dialogue** (all levels). Take a simple narrative, cut into equal sentences or parts and give each member of a group one part. Students must read their part for a few minutes, without showing the others, and then return the slip of paper to the teacher. Now students use their memory and own language and collaborate with the aim of fitting together the story. They then either retell it orally or write it up as a group. This works well with higher level groups if you choose a text on an issue that can be divided into three or four parts. Students then collaborate to summarise the ideas found in their part and decide who had the introduction, conclusion, etc.

> Here is a very simple one suggested by Michael Swan called
> *The Penguin*. Can you find the correct order?
>
> The policeman was very surprised and said: '*Didn't I tell you to take him to the zoo.*'
> He found a penguin.
> The policeman told John to take it to the zoo.
> John was walking down the street one day when …
> He didn't know what to do so he stopped a policeman.
> John said: '*Yes, we went to the zoo yesterday and now we are going to the cinema*'.
> The next day the policeman met John in the street with the penguin.

Preparing students for discussion
pp 50–1

Handling discussion
p 53

Discussion or debates in groups
pp 52–3

Communication games
pp 96–7

Role play: fluency tasks

**Role play
from texts**
p 53

Role play requires students to:

- take on a role (imagine they are someone else)

- imagine a situation (pretend they are in another time and place)

- improvise in their choice of language.

**Role play
from songs**
p 88

**The learner's
world**
pp 52, 94, 110

Some people find their new *persona* liberating, others find pretending to be embarrassing. It is a good way for learners to try out their knowledge and improve fluency in a classroom situation. This type of activity maximises students' talking time and also appeals to shy students who do not like performing in front of a whole class, but can express themselves in the relative privacy of a small group. However, reading a set dialogue is not role play. Many role plays are based on cards or situations described by the teacher.

> Example: Student A – *'You have just arrived home an hour later than your parents allow. Your father is waiting for you at the door. Act out the conversation you have with your father. Student B is your father/mother.'*

The best types of role play

- Draw on students' own experience of the world. It is difficult for teenagers to imagine themselves in many work situations (although they probably would be able to play a shop assistant).

- Draw on situations they are likely to find themselves in when they are travelling and/or meeting English speakers.

- Draw on familiar characters from school, home, their textbook or maybe television.

'... some classes quite like doing role plays to illustrate a certain point, e.g. smoking. A parent has found a packet of fags in their child's room, and one takes the part of the parent, one the child.' **Caroline O'Shaughnessy, e-mailed to the Germany assistants discussion group**.

Tips on the management of role play

- **Keep a low profile**. There is nothing worse than a teacher breathing down your neck. Keep a distance to give them freedom to experiment.

- **Listen carefully**. Note down relevant aspects of the students' use of language and creativity, which you can highlight to them afterwards. Note errors but only major ones. If you take notes don't do it so obviously that you look like a detective. It puts students off.

- **Try not to intervene**. Respond to requests from students for help, or intervene if there has been a breakdown in communication and the role play needs to be put back on course.

- **Keep instructions clear and concise**. If it takes an age to explain it is too complicated.

- **Demonstrate (rehearse)** the role play before students start by themselves.

- **Don't force shy students to perform** in front of the whole class.

Error correction techniques pp 28–32

Free role plays

These can be more challenging without the support of an example dialogue or text. The language is decided by the students but needs careful preparation. Brainstorm with the whole class and give pairs or groups plenty of time to plan and practise.

Learner-generated tasks pp 96–7, 99–101

'The teacher of my year 9 class approached me and said he wanted to practise their use of everyday English, i.e. going to a chemist [...] so I made a few scenarios which can be cut up and laminated on to cards, etc. First of all the students got all four sheets and had the chance to read them through and explain any words they didn't know. Then they had to choose one scenario and [...] go through them with me which only takes two to three minutes each. Afterwards I wrote a few pointers on how they did for a feedback session later. Next week [...] the teacher wants to videotape it.

The thing that is important about these lessons is that these scenarios are things that could really come up – they are REAL so if students can do these it can work wonders for their self confidence'. **Suzannah McDonnell, Hessen, mailed to the Germany assistants discussion group**.

Unit 5 Conversation and discussion with texts

We very rarely enter a discussion without some previous knowledge of the subject matter or some forewarning so that we can prepare ourselves mentally or take notes. The key to successful exploitation of a text for discussion lies in the preparation of the text, the time given to students to prepare what they have to say and the type of conversation tasks given. We cannot just assume, even with fairly proficient students, that the subject matter of the text will be so gripping that they will naturally launch into a heated debate on the subject.

Working with the class teacher

It can be useful to consider the following questions:

Speaking skills –
free practice and
controlled practice
pp 37–43

- **How much practice have students had in debating or discussing in pairs?** Sometimes the assistant is asked to hold conversation classes, of which discussion based on a text may be a part, with students who are unused to working freely in pairs or in small groups. You will need to take extra care in preparing them and giving them controlled discussion tasks to guide their conversations if they are not used to working freely.

Planning schemes
of work
pp 6–7

- **What sort of discussion tasks are provided in the main textbook** used by the teacher? Get a copy of the book and liaise with the teacher to talk about the activities he or she finds appropriate or successful. This may indicate which text types will be suitable for your group. It also means you benefit from the teacher's knowledge of the students. Try to create a coherent link between the students' main textbook and the work they do with you.

Working with
teachers
pp 3–8

- **Can the text you use be linked to the main language work in the textbook** covered by the teacher? Keep an eye on what types of themes or topics are covered in the main textbook. For example, students have recently covered the language function of suggestions with the use of *'Why don't we ...?' 'I think we should ..., etc.'* Your discussion task could involve students in suggesting a course of action, solving a problem and suggesting solutions. Don't forget that your role is often to provide further opportunities for language use of items recently covered in the syllabus.

Tips on choosing a text

- **Length**. The main aim is to generate free conversation or discussion. If your text is very lengthy and takes a good deal of time to wade through, there will be no time for much discussion. Short and succinct can be best. For example, a three-paragraph newspaper article, four or five comments by teenagers posted on-line during a debate, or a very funny short story with an unexpected ending.

- **Visual support**. It helps to set the context and prepare vocabulary if the text has a good supporting photograph or two.

- **Relevance to students**. Consider the age and also the experience of the students. Can they relate to the topic or is it too adult? They will have more ideas and opinions if they get personally involved.

- **Balance**. Vary your choice of text from serious to funny, though not so wacky that the students will miss the point – much humour is culture bound. However, a debate on ways to curb teenage smoking, based on advertisements or an article, can be followed in a later lesson with a lighter topic related to music or fashion.

- **Linguistic relevance**. Have students got the necessary vocabulary and language to cope successfully with the topic? No matter how interesting, they may be lost for words and demotivated by a demanding text.

Using visuals
pp 68–79

Language level and
speaking skills
pp 36–8

Texts for discussion: teen magazine example

Key features of a suitable text:

- not too long

- clear ideas and balanced arguments

- relevant to secondary school students

- gives some cultural background

- visuals and a headline which help preparation

- lends itself easily to a discussion task.

Teens turn to work

*We all remember with fondness or horror our first Saturday
job at thirteen or fourteen. Mine was in a department store and
it gave me just enough money to pay for the pop concerts and latest
fashions I read about in teen mags. Whilst Saturday jobs continue to
be extremely popular with British and American teenagers, there is a
new breed of worker on the scene. Not content to just work on
Saturdays, some American teens are working late afternoons and on
into the evenings. Recent research indicates that some young people
work as many as thirty hours a week in low-paid service sector jobs.
Teachers are increasingly concerned that this pressure to work is
having a negative effect on their school work.*

*The cost of long-term education in the States means that some families
have great difficulty paying university fees and expenses. More and
more young Americans are starting jobs well before they finish
High School and this helps them save up for university. Added to this
economic reality is the growing independence of young spenders.
A lot of teenagers on both sides of the Atlantic like earning their own
spending money, rather than asking their parents. This extra work is*

Among high school students in the United States aged fifteen to eighteen,
seventy-one per cent have had a job and forty-one per cent say they are
currently employed.

Hours per week students say they work:

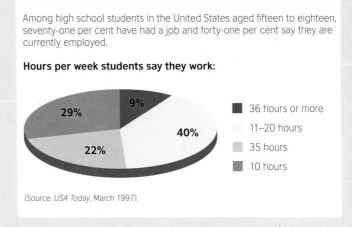

- 36 hours or more
- 11–20 hours
- 35 hours
- 10 hours

9%
40%
22%
29%

[Source: *USA Today*, March 1997]

*easier to fit into studies in America where the system is more flexible
than in Europe. There are greater chances to catch up than in European
or Asian systems, the system is less demanding and competitive and
there are far more low-paid part-time jobs on offer in America.*

*Across the Atlantic most British teenagers still stick to the Saturday job
tradition because the school day during the week is so long and the
amount of homework so great. Increasing numbers are looking for
summer jobs which are still difficult to find if you are under eighteen.
British university students are, however, waking up to the realities
faced by young Americans and are sometimes forced to seek
part-time work during term-time to meet living expenses. The days of
a little Saturday job for spending money and a few years at university
supported by the government and your parents are long gone.*

Techniques for preparing the text and topic

All of the techniques listed below aim to make the text as accessible as possible so that students can get to the meaning and main ideas quickly. Texts intended as a stimulus for discussion should not turn into lengthy reading comprehension tasks. They should serve as a vehicle for giving students time to think of a topic, preview the relevant vocabulary, talk about it and share their ideas with their classmates.

Using photos
pp 77–8, 98

• **Use any visuals for vocabulary brainstorming**.

Example: Think of five words related to the photo or anticipate the main message of the text through careful questioning: *'Where is the girl in the picture? How old do you think she is? Why do you think she is working there?'* All this elicits useful vocabulary and prepares students for the content of the text.

Using newspapers
pp 123–5

• **Use any headlines or sub-headings**. Write these on the board before showing the text. Ask students to guess what the article is about.

Example: *What type of work do you think will be described in the text ? Think of another way of saying 'turn to'.*

• **Use key words**. Take five or six key words from the text and put them on the board before students read the text.

Example: *Saturday job   save up   part-time   university fees
pocket money   low-paid*

After reading, ask students to look at the words again and verbally summarise the message of the text using the words as prompts. This gives students time to think and to practise making sentences about the topic.

**Questionnaires
in speaking skills
lessons**
p 41

• **Use questionnaires**. Give students a mini-questionnaire related to the theme of the text before they read it.

Example: *Do you get any pocket money or monthly allowance? Have you ever worked to earn money? What type of things do you use your spending money for?*

- **Use prediction exercises**. Involve students in a prediction exercise to anticipate the vocabulary and ideas of the text. This helps them to read the text with real interest.

Techniques for developing cultural competence pp 105–9

> Example: *Which of these statements about American and British teenagers is likely to be true? Read the text and check your predictions.*
>
> *'Most British teenagers have no time for extra paid work during term-time because the school day is long.'*
>
> *'British and American teenagers like to have Saturday jobs.'*
>
> *'Jobs for students in the US are generally well paid.'*
>
> *'Some American teenagers work as many as thirty hours a week when they are at school.'*
>
> *'University students in the UK do not work during their studies.'*
>
> *'Many university students in the United States have term-time jobs to pay for college fees and living expenses.'*

> Another prediction technique based on the text:
> *Here are some of the possible reasons why American teenagers work during term-time. Tick those reasons which seem most likely – decide in pairs.*
>
> *'They only go to school in the mornings.'*
>
> *'They don't get any homework so have lots of free time.'*
>
> *'They need to save up for college which can be very expensive.'*
>
> *'They don't always like asking their parents for money.'*
>
> *'It is easy to catch up if you miss school because courses are flexible.'*

Types of discussion task based on a text

The degree of control needed in your discussion task very much depends on the language level of students. A class may not be able to cope with a full-scale debate but they might be able to discuss their opinions with the help of a questionnaire which guides them. One of the main reasons that discussions dry up or become too teacher-led is because students lack control of the language needed to discuss the topic. The tasks outlined below provide students

Fluency practice pp 41–5

Speaking skills
p 36

with a linguistic framework and some of the words they need are embedded in the task. They also provide a framework for the content, acting as a plan to give the discussion structure. While open, general chats with large groups can bring up interesting points and provide moments of real debate, more structured tasks ensure that all students are involved in talking. In addition, decision-making approaches involve an element of negotiation with your partner or group and this in turn generates more opportunities for the conversational management skills needed by learners.

In short, it is not simply enough to read a text and then ask students: *What do you think?*

- **Personalise the topic**.

> Example: *Here are some of the types of Saturday jobs that UK teenagers do: working in a record shop; working in a clothes shop; serving in a fast food restaurant; delivering papers or other literature to homes; filling supermarket shelves with stock; helping in a public library; helping in a local community centre.*
> *a) Which job would you prefer? Tell your group why.*
> *b) Put the jobs in order of the best paid and worst paid. Do you all agree?*

- **Extend the topic to involve students' experience and knowledge of the world**.

The student's own culture
p 110

> Example: *Work experience, work placements and careers visits to industry are part of the school curriculum in the US and the UK. Look at this list of school subjects. Decide what types of work experience or visits could be done in your region. Present your findings to the class.*
> Biology; information technology; history; foreign languages.

- **Provide students with a ranking task where they have to agree on an order**.

> Example: *Which of these factors do you think employers rate the most highly in choosing a student to employ?*
> Enthusiasm; willingness to work for low wages; academic ability; previous work experience; availability.

Another variation on ranking is to give the class three short CVs for three secondary school students. In groups they decide which student should get a holiday job you have specified.

- **Provide a task for controlled debating**. Give students a list of opinions *for and against*, e.g. in the case of *Teens turn to work*, arguments for and against school students working during term-time. Students then work in pairs saying which opinions they agree or disagree with and why.

  'A job teaches young people the value of work.'

  'No child should be allowed to work – it's cruel.'

  'All teenagers should have some experience of the real world before leaving school.'

  'If young people have to work it's because their parents are too mean to give them spending money.'

  Alternatively ask one pair of students to prepare arguments in favour of young people earning during term-time and another pair prepare arguments against. Then bring the pairs together. Each side has to support its position.

- **Devise a role play situation linked to the topic**. Divide the class into two groups – employers and candidates for a part-time job. Employers prepare questions and candidates anticipate the questions and prepare their answers. Put each employer with one candidate to simulate a job interview. Put prompts on the board to help them formulate their questions and answers. *Pay? Experience? Hours? Availability? Job responsibilities?*

Role play
pp 44–5

Classroom management and feedback

Discussions in pairs or small groups give students far more talking practice than teacher-led discussions. However, it is sometimes very tempting for teachers to intervene if a discussion seems to be flagging only to end up dominating the process and doing all the talking. We need to see our role as guides who support the students' practice.

- Provide language prompts on the board or on small cards for students to refer to, e.g. expressions for agreement, disagreement, asking for clarification, etc.

- If students need further suggestions for ideas or they are having trouble finding the right words to express a point, intervene in their pair or small group briefly to help them continue talking.

Error correction
pp 28–34

- While you go around listening to students, encourage them with praise for both their language use and their ideas. Make a mental note of any recurring difficulties which are common to the whole class.

- Make time at the end of the lesson to follow up the discussions and conclude. Firstly give praise and encouragement for students' efforts and ideas, ask group leaders to summarise their group or pair conclusions. If time is short you can summarise what you have heard.

**Working with the
class teacher**
pp 6–8

- If you find, during a discussion session, that a lot of students are unsure of a grammatical point covered in their main syllabus, this may be because they are so new to it that they are still in need of a lot of practice to gain more accuracy. It may be helpful to alert their class teacher, who can then integrate revision of the language point in the scheme of work.

Resources for texts

Internet resources
pp 133–5

The Internet has certainly revolutionised the access all teachers and assistants have to a wealth of texts around the English-speaking world. The example used in this chapter is from a teen magazine but it is only one text type of many. For example, a traveller's tale with an element of adventure or amusing outcome can stimulate discussion. True but unusual tales about people and their everyday lives can be thought-provoking. Some sources of texts are listed below:

Published resources
pp 135–7

- **The international press** (also readily available on-line). The young people's versions are a good source for content and also length, e.g. *Time for Kids*, the *Electronic Telegraph*.

- **Teen publications and magazines** (including those on-line) cover issues and also events in the cultural calendar of teenagers around the world. Look out for topics that relate to a season, e.g. Christmas, end of year exams, high school proms, summer holidays or the latest crazes or fashions that interest your students.

- **On-line debates and discussion groups** for young people can provide a selection of e-mailed opinions, often in response to a short news item of relevance to young people. Similar vox-pop style reports are always in the popular press, women's magazines and publications for young people.

- **Language-learning magazines** such as those published by MGP International.

Tip: If you find a relevant text, but it is too demanding linguistically, modify it to suit the level of the class.

The best texts for generating conversation

- texts outlining the main points of an issue or topic

- a dilemma or problem for which students can suggest advice, a solution or a possible outcome.

- a narrative which encourages prediction of what might happen next.

- a situation which encourages hypothesis, e.g. *What would you do if ...?*

- a description of life or people in the past which can be compared to the present.

Unit 6 Speech work

What does speech work involve?

Fluency
versus accuracy
p 28

- **The physical ability to articulate sounds**. Motor skills, such as where to put the tongue and lips to produce the English consonant cluster /θ/ as in *thank you, three, thirteen*.

- **The ability to get your message across**. Accurate and fluent control of the language.

- **The ability to convey attitude**. Stress and intonation carry meaning, e.g. *Yes?* (rising pitch for a question) and *Yes* (downward pitch for affirmative).

- **The ability to be a good listener**. Not sounding as if you are interrogating a person, using listener tactics to show interest, such as *mmmm; yes; really?; you're joking!*

Getting the mechanics right – pronunciation practice

Authentic listening
pp 82–3

Bad pronunciation can be a serious problem if it negatively affects understanding, but we do not need to aim for native-speaker perfection. There is nothing wrong with sounding foreign, but it is important to be intelligible. Pronunciation is closely linked to the ear, and listening is a vital part of developing this area. Listening to a model on tape, CD or video, or using your own voice as a model will be the most effective way of doing this. Teachers will call upon you as a model, in some cases very frequently. You need to recognise the value of being a native speaker of English and exploit it well to assist non-native teachers and their students. Where possible use picture prompts and other visual materials (rather than the written word) in your pronunciation teaching, unless you are looking at the sentence stress system. This is because the spaces between words in English are different in written form from spoken form. Reading individual words we wish students to hear is a distraction and this may break the flow of sounds. Example: News item = *new͜zitem*; He's a doctor = *He's͜ə doctor*; How do you do? = *How dyu do?*

'Listen and repeat' is the best model to follow.

Tips for achieving a good model of spoken English

- **Speed**. Don't change, keep to a fairly normal speed but pause a little longer between sense groups. The learners' ears have to tune in to your voice and this will take time. Slowing down too much will only distort the sound you are modelling.

- **Consistency**. Don't change your intonation. This is easier said than done if you are not used to modelling intonation. One tip is to break your model by giving a brief command to the class which then helps you to repeat the item, e.g. *'What's your name?' 'Listen again / all together / What's your name?'*

- **Variety**. Use a good balance of whole class or choral responses and individual repetition.

- **Listening**. Move around and listen to individuals. Try to be silent when students are speaking so that you can listen to them. When students repeat, don't repeat with them.

- **Frequency**. It is better to do five minutes of speech work every lesson than one long session every now and then. Pronunciation practice can be boring and repetitive if you do it for a long time.

- **Clarity**. Make every possible use of visual clues to help students. Speak clearly, facing them so they can all see your mouth and facial expression. When using video, exploit the video with sound off, asking questions about the speaker's mood (e.g. *'Is he angry?' 'Friendly?'*) and body language, before showing the video with sound on.

Using English in class
pp 16, 25–6

Reading aloud for sense groups
p 66

Classroom management
pp 17–23

Using video
pp 89–91

Ear training

Pronunciation
and different
nationalities
p 130

One important part of pronunciation practice is helping students make sense of the fuzz they may perceive when listening to spoken English. This can be done by sensitising the ear. Our ears will pick up sounds similar to those in our own language but might not hear sounds from another. We need plenty of repetition, pronunciation practice and ear training. For example, Spanish speakers have difficulty hearing the difference between /b/ and /v/ in English. Similarly, German speakers have difficulty hearing the difference between /v/ and /w/. The *'th'* sounds (i.e. /ð/ as in *they* and /θ/ as in *think*) do not exist in French or Italian, so learners don't know where to put their lips, teeth or tongues to form the sound!

Minimal pairs

Pronunciation
resources
p 137

It will not be sufficient to just hear the sound that is new, it needs to be compared and contrasted with the sound from the students' own language which is mistaken for it. This involves creating minimal pairs of sounds to highlight the differences in, e.g. *ship/sheep*; *fit/feet*, since the sound /ɪ/ in the English *ship* and *fit* does not feature in Spanish, French or Italian and is substituted with /i/ as in *sheep* and *feet*. Consonant clusters beginning with /θ/ are a problem for Germans, Spanish, French and Italians. Minimal pair work can contrast /θ/ in *three* with the /t/ as in *tree*.

Minimal pair tasks – when and how

It is best to deal with minimal pair work when it arises out of a real need. It can be a mistake to identify sounds which cause bother for the learners in your host country and then introduce activities out of the blue that bear no relation to the rest of the lesson. If a problem arises during a class with a teacher and you are asked to model a consonant or vowel, then it is an appropriate moment to give a set of minimal pairs to illustrate the sound, so have a list prepared wherever possible.

Games for ear training

- **The same or different?**

  – Prepare a list of minimal pairs, e.g. *hit/heat, bit/beat, sit/seat, grin/green, tin/teen.*

  – Read out one pair and get students to say which word is each, writing them on board.

  – Read one of the words twice. *'Are they the same or different?'* (The same.)

  – Read the contrasting words. *'Are they the same or different?'* (Different.)

  – Continue with all the pairs, mixing same and different. Students write S or D in their notebooks.

  – Pairs can confer and then read the list of pairs again for checking.

  Alternatively, make it into a team challenge game. Doing this with numbers from the beginning is great fun, e.g. *'13 or 30? 14 or 40?'* and numbers which cause confusion, such as 6 and 7 in combinations 66 or 67.

- **Minimal pair pictures**. With younger learners the minimal pair listening can become a drawing exercise. Either circle the drawing if you hear the word, e.g. house or *mouse* or ask a class to draw the word they hear and compare drawings to check.

- **Odd man out**. Read a list of four words, all except one containing the same consonant cluster or vowel. *'Was it 1, 2, 3, or 4?'* For example, church; shoe; chess; cheese.

- **How many times?** Choose a sound to focus on and after initial repetition read sentences or a short text containing the sound once, twice or even three times. Teams must say if they have heard it more than once or just once. Pick some sentences where the sound is not there at all!

Using visual aids
pp 68–79

Making repetition fun

Repetition of phrases and words is a necessary part of language learning. Teenagers are the most reticent group of learners, since they are more concerned with making fools of themselves in front of their peers. Making repetition into a fun activity, and not a chore, can be done in a variety of ways.

Reading aloud
and oral exams
p 66

- **Play with volume**. Ask learners to say something in a louder voice, increasing the volume (be wary of the classes next door) or ask students to speak in a whisper, very quietly.

- **Experiment with tone**. Say something in a curious, surprised, angry, bored or frightened tone. This is great for raising awareness of intonation and its importance. Even beginners' classes enjoy experimenting with different ways of asking *Yes?* or saying *Thank you*. This is also useful for higher level students preparing for reading aloud in exams.

- **Experiment with speed**. *'How fast can you say it?'*, building up speed like a train.

- **Adding to a list** (see list games for practising unstressed syllables below) and making it into a game-like activity: *'We went to the park and we played tennis, played football, played cards on the grass, played ...'*

- **Playing with numbers**. Counting in evens, odds, tens, backwards or saying times tables. (If you have younger learners and beginners use maths chants and times tables to music – there are lots of CDs available in the UK.) Look at alphabet games used in UK primary schools for more inspiration.

Games
pp 92–101

- **Playing with rhyme**. Play rhyme games, where one student says a word and the next adds one that rhymes, e.g. day ... play ... say ... pay ... grey

- **Categorise words**. Mix up groups of words with contrasting vowels or consonants which cause difficulty with different stress patterns. Students in pairs divide the words into two or three categories and then listen to check. Repeat the words with the class. Students think of more words to fit each category.

Raps, chants and songs for repetition

Jazz chants have been very successfully used in ELT. Songs based on repetition of items or a distinctive refrain can work well from beginners upwards, such as traditional songs like 'Ten green bottles', 'There was an old woman who swallowed a fly' or pop songs which appeal to the age range.

Using songs
pp 85–8

The stress system: weak forms and the schwa /ə/

The most important sound in the English language is the schwa /ə/. Note its presence in the following basic exchanges: *'Have you got thə time?' 'Yes, it's nine ə'clock.'* This neutral vowel is used in unstressed syllables of words and weak forms in a sentence. It should be a priority to help students become aware of this throughout their course, from beginners up to advanced level. This weak vowel-sound /ə/ can replace every vowel sound and so has its own symbol. If you wish to teach any symbols this one should be the main one. Word stress in English is variable: any syllable can carry the main stress whereas in other languages stress may fall on the last syllable, so learners are surprised. Getting the stress on the wrong syllable can make the word incomprehensible to native English speakers. This has more impact on intelligibility than mispronounced sounds. In sentences the stress of words shifts according to meaning. (Note the stress shifts. On the unstressed word the vowel sound becomes a schwa.)

Pronunciation resources
p 137

Explaining the meaning of new words
p 125

Who are you waiting **for**?
I'm waiting fə my sister.

Where are you **from**?
I'm frəm Spain.

Awareness activities for the stress system

Work on recognising weak forms helps students to hear unstressed elements in speech and greatly improves listening comprehension. From beginner level upwards, five-minute activities to integrate with all lessons:

- **Counting syllables** (on fingers) through listening, not looking at words.

- **Dividing a sentence into groups** of syllables through listening.

- **Practising with visuals of two-syllable words** with stress on the first syllable, e.g. Germən, and sets like: mother, father, sister, brother; doctor, teacher, driver, baker; better, faster, cheaper.

Controlled practice
pp 37–41

- **Listening and practice with sentences** (long and short) with articles *a* and *an*, as well as *and*. Lists, shopping, ordering in a café, telling the time.

  Example: The weak vowel in ten-ə-clock, ten-tə-ten. Isolate sentence groups for quick controlled practice before speaking tasks like role plays.

  Example: Note the unstressed article and linking in this group. ə cupəv coffee; ə glassəv milk; ə pieceəv cake; ə sliceəv tart

  Example: Play a list game chorally round the class. The first student starts: *'I'd like a cup of coffee please.'* The next student adds: *'I'd like a cup of coffee and a sandwich please.'* The next student adds: *'I'd like a cup of coffee, a sandwich and a glass of water please.'* Play the game in the same way with other situations: *'What did John take on holiday to the Sahara?'* or *'What did Peter give his ten girlfriends on Valentine's Day?'*

- **Look at syllables and stress** in a wide variety of words and sentences as well as short paragraphs.

Planning with
the textbook
p 7

- **Use familiar textbook dialogues**. Ask students to highlight the words which they think are the most important parts of communication. Listen and check how much these words are stressed. This sentence focus is beneficial for listening skills as students identify the main message.

Newspapers and
vocabulary
pp 124–5

- **Encourage students to anticipate the pronunciation** of new words encountered in reading and mark the stress of new words when you write them on the board. If dictionaries are used, draw attention to stress markings in students' dictionaries.

Using songs
pp 85–8

- **Use songs**. Sentence stress and the schwa /ə/ are usually very clear in songs. Singers greatly exaggerate stressed syllables and the contrast is more marked. Use individual singers with strong, clear voices. Integrate this aspect with your other exploitation tasks for songs.

Using newspapers
pp 123–5

- **Use newspaper headlines**. Headlines are created by reducing the message of a sentence to the key words, which are those which are stressed. Contrasting a headline with its complete message highlights the stress patterns of English.

Linkage of sounds

When listening to English at normal speed you will note that we move smoothly from one word to the next, so that there aren't pauses between words. This can be seen in the most basic expressions: *Thanks a lot*. (*Thanksə* sounds like a single, two-syllable word), and the most elementary of sentences: *I'm a student* (*I'mə ...*). Pausing after every word sounds artificial. Indicate linkage in board summaries for all classes.

Treat groups of words and phrases as they come up in a course:

- could have = couldəv; must have = mustəv; might have = mightəv; two weeks ago = two weeksəgo; three years ago = three yearsəgo

- the linking /r/ in: here and there; better and better; closer and closer; mother and father.

Tasks for awareness of linking (all levels)

- **Focus on a sentence or question type** and give six to eight examples. Students in pairs decide which words the speaker might link and then listen to check. E.g. *'Will you be coming tomorrow? I'll see if I can get there by six. What will you do if she doesn't ring? I'll go by myself.'*

- **Take a very short passage**, one paragraph, which is easy for students to understand. Ask students to listen and mark any points where words are linked. Go through with the class, listen again, ask for repetition. Pairs then practise reading aloud to each other. Do the same with short dialogues.

Intonation

Intonation is very important for intelligibility since it tells the listener something about the speaker's intentions. Misunderstanding can occur when you might think a speaker sounds bored when there isn't the same use of pitch or variation in melody in the voice in their own language. Link your intonation practice to the functional use of language in the students' course. Take short dialogues from their textbook or a video clip of one brief exchange in order to focus on one feature.

Information gap
for oral practice
p 40

Example: Asking for repetition: listen and read. Notice where the voice rises or falls. Then listen and repeat.

A: What time's the Amsterdam train? ↘   A: How far is it to Amsterdam? ↘

B: Eleven   B: About 200 km

A: Sorry? ↗ What time? ↗   A: How far? ↗

B: Eleven, eleven in the morning. ↘   B: About 200 km ↘

Follow up choral repetition with controlled pair practice. Students use two different maps of Europe with distances and timetables.

The assistant as visual aid p 68

Using the board well pp 68–71

Tips for dealing with intonation

- **The pitch movement** at the end of a sentence or question is essential for meaning and understanding the speaker's attitude. Focus on this clearly.

- **Try not to use very long examples** for practice, as students find it difficult.

- **Use your hands as a conductor** to show sweep and flow of pitch as you ask a question for speech practice. Keep these hand movements consistent.

- **Use arrows on the board** to highlight pitch rising or falling.

- **Use backchaining**: read long sentences down from the end to help students repeat them, e.g. 'Do you mind if I smoke?' Do this in a lively, brisk manner.

Assistant: *smoke?*	Students: *smoke?*
Assistant: *if I smoke?*	Students: *if I smoke?*
Assistant: *mind if I smoke?*	Students: *mind if I smoke?*
Assistant: *Do you mind if I smoke?*	Students: *Do you mind if I smoke?*

Integrating speech work with class work

- **Liaise with the main teacher** so that you can anticipate useful work, even at beginner level.

- **Check the pronunciation work in course books**. What is it like? Does the class teacher use it? Could it be of use for you to cover it? In a very busy school year with little contact time for English, pronunciation work might be viewed by some teachers as a luxury they haven't time for.

- **Make time for a little speech work in all your lessons**. E.g. if students will be working on the simple past in coursebook lessons, involve them in a discrimination game with regular past tense '-ed' endings.

> *Listen to the verbs from the dialogue/in these sentences. Do they end with the sounds /t/ or /id/ or /d/?'* Incorporate the verbs into a past tense bingo game. (Wash/t/, watch/t/, visit/id/, wait/id/, arriv/d/)

Planning work
with textbooks
p 7

- **Focus on intonation** depending on the functional language of their main textbook. Re-use short known dialogues from their books. This means you can completely focus on intonation, without worrying about them not understanding the dialogue.

- **If you are team-teaching, insist that you have forewarning** of any dialogues that might be used. Show the teacher why you might be of help by highlighting the intonation features.

Working well with teachers

Team teaching
pp 6–8

Warning. Over-enthusiasm can sometimes be perceived by teachers as a sign that you are taking over. This is regrettable and is compounded when assistants complain that they are not given enough responsibility. In a team teaching situation the assistant is fulfilling a useful role as a good model for pronunciation and as a reference for teachers. If you find yourself working together with teachers in the classroom, accept this helping role and try to make it as successful as possible. Try to be helpful in pinpointing areas of speech work for short practice. Arm yourself with good, practical reference material about your language. You will be used more if you prove yourself to be a useful and willing resource. Some assistants find that teachers criticise their accent because they have less experience of the range of UK accents. Reassure the teacher that your way of speaking is perfectly acceptable.

Establishing a
working relationship
with teachers
pp 5–8

Building resources
pp 126–7

Unit 7 Visual aids

The assistant as visual aid

Gesture in
error correction
p 30

Your facial expression, gestures and mimes can greatly enhance students' understanding of your meaning. Without turning into an absolute clown you can take steps to help students understand by:

Getting used to
classroom language
pp 16, 25–6

• miming the action you are describing, e.g. when students are first getting used to classroom instructions in English: *'Listen carefully'* (teacher points to ear), *'You've got five minutes'* (teacher points to watch and shows five fingers)

• exaggerating your facial expressions slightly to get across a sense of mood – surprise, disapproval

Using video
pp 89–91

This can be compared to listening to the radio or watching a video of the same conversation. The facial expressions and gestures in video help learners arrive at meaning while with radio it is harder with no visual clues.

The blackboard/whiteboard

Clarifying meaning
with time-lines
p 34

This is your main piece of equipment in most schools and it is vital that you use it well. Not every school provides unlimited access to photocopiers! However, the amount of English acquired by students is not linked to the amount of equipment at the teacher's disposal. So don't despair if you have little more than a blackboard to work with.

Board uses

Discipline problems
pp 21–3

The board is for drawing students' attention to new language, checking understanding and summarising your lesson. Consider that what you write on it and how you write it will be copied into notebooks and imprinted on students' minds. It therefore needs to be uncluttered, well organised and useful for study purposes. Random jottings which end up covering the whole board are not effective. We also need to practise writing clearly and simply on the board, in a straight line, large enough to be seen at the back. Disruption is caused during classes when pupils can't read or understand your notes and when you spend too much time at the board without involving them. The two key factors are presentation/layout and organised and selective content.

Do	Don't
maintain eye contact with the class while writing, standing sideways without hiding what you are writing.	write with your back to the class in silence (as students can take this as a chance to chatter).
write as quickly and clearly as you can. Limit the length of texts or instructions. If possible, prepare a text beforehand if you have access to an empty room.	spend a long time at the board (as it can cause boredom and disruption).
while writing, keep their attention by reading key words and phrases and getting choral repetition at each pause.	hide what you are writing with your body. fail to involve students.
tell students at which point you want them to copy, such as at the end. *'Don't copy this yet. You can when I have finished'* or *'This is on your handout. Don't copy it'*. remember to stand back and give them time to copy.	start writing with no instructions to the class (otherwise they will try to copy, not listen and struggle to see what you are doing).
divide the board into distinct sections with the centre for main structures or language points, one side margin for key vocabulary and a space for temporary items (to rub out as you go along). select only the important points.	write everything that crops up in the lesson so the board becomes overcrowded and messy (this leads to disorganised note-taking – no matter how much you tell students not to copy everything, they will think it is all vital).

Variety of pace
pp 17–18

Classroom management
pp 20–3

Grading your language
pp 16, 25, 56–7

Projector uses:

- **Layering or building**: reveal information slowly by preparing one picture or table. Add further details to the picture on a separate slide which you lie on top of the first.

  Example: Students draw a picture of an empty beach as in your first slide. Students listen/read a description of the beach and add details or teacher dictates details:

  'There's a man fishing in the rock pool. There are two boys playing football near the kiosk.'

  Students check their effort with your second slide which reveals all the details.

- **Text work with the whole class**.

  Example: Show students a whole page of blanks. Each blank represents a word in the story. Students start with nothing except a title, e.g. *'Angry girlfriend calls the speaking clock'*. Students must then predict words as quickly as possible and build up the story piece by piece. As more items are added, missing parts are guessed from context. Give students place names and names of people. First suggestions might be: girlfriend, he, she, a, the, telephone, etc.

  Text example:

  A man had an argument with his girlfriend. The next day he went away for work and didn't come back for a week. When he returned he found that his telephone was off the hook. His girlfriend had left a note for him next to the telephone. The note read: 'I'm leaving you, goodbye.' He picked up the telephone and listened. It was the speaking clock in New York!

Flashcards

After making very colourful flashcards for key topics and lexical sets, it is easy to under-use them. The advantages of flashcards are:

1 You can use them as an introduction/warm-up to reactivate students' language.

- Get students in pairs to guess the words or phrases that the pictures represent.

- Make a team game. Partially cover each picture (with black card with a shaped cut-out which gives a keyhole effect) and challenge teams to guess the word. Further points can be added or gained by making a sentence about the picture or asking a question about it.

- You can use sets of pictures and ask what they have in common, e.g. all modes of transport; all objects you might find in a bedroom; all uncountable foodstuffs; all countries in the Southern Hemisphere; all spare time activities, etc.

2 You can use the flashcards as cues for substitution in dialogues, e.g. a lexical set of pictures of drinks on the board.

Teacher offers the drinks: *'Would you like a cup of tea? sugar? some milk?'* Students respond and continue practising: *'Yes, please.'* The teacher then elicits questions from students using the cards and invites others to respond. The dialogue can be further refined until the flashcards serve as prompts for students working alone.

Small cards

Nearly all the activities possible with a whole class using a flashcard or set of flashcards can also be done as a card game with students working in pairs or small groups. See above and Unit 9 for card games with pictures and words.

Posters and flipcharts

You can prepare posters or flipcharts for the classroom. Keep them large, simple and clear, with not too much information. The following posters can be useful: classroom instructions; classroom requests; language tables.

Sources of pictures
for flashcards
p 128

Setting up games
pp 93–4

Controlled oral work
pp 37–41

Eliciting dialogue
p 39

Setting up
card games
pp 95–6

Resources for
free posters
p 129

Pictures, photos and postcards

Using one large picture

Two types of picture:
1 a scene with lots happening in it
2 one simple picture of a street; room; house.

Fig. 2 **taken from *Elementary communication games* – Jill Hadfield, Longman ELT**

Different task types

- *'Describe what you can see.'*

- *'Find someone who is ...'*

- Dictation: *'Listen and colour,'* or *'Add things to your picture'.*

- Vocabulary searches: *'Find five things beginning with "s". Write all the verbs to describe what is happening.'*

- Memory: *'Look at the picture for five minutes and answer your partner's questions, e.g. Is there a man sitting in a deckchair? How many people are playing with the beach ball?'*

Using two very similar pictures

These could illustrate: rooms; people; machines; busy scenes (e.g. airport, classroom).

This works very well with the whole class or pairs working back to back so that they cannot see each others' picture, and have to ask questions to find differences or exchange details.

Fig. 3 **taken from _Play games with English 1_ – Colin Granger, Macmillan Heinemann**

(illustration by John Plum)

Different task types

1 Spot the difference

Find four differences between your suitcase and your partner's by asking questions: *'Have you got a hair brush in your case?' 'Have you got any shoes?' 'Is the mirror in your room round?' 'No, it's square.'*

Using information
gap activities
p 40

2 Find the missing things to complete a picture

It is best if both the pictures provided have missing objects. This means that both students have to ask questions to arrive at a complete picture. Students ask each other directions to complete a map. Students have a list of objects and ask questions to draw them into their picture: *'Have you seen my pen?' 'Yes, it's over there on top of the television.'* You can do these activities with a whole class too. The teacher has the main picture and the students have to complete theirs.

Using a sequence of pictures which represent a story

These are useful for practice in describing events, past, present or future.

Different task types (small groups/pairs/individuals or whole class)

1 Students re-order the pictures into a coherent story and then tell it orally.

Fig. 4 **Sequence of pictures**

2 Students each have a different picture in a four-part story.
All four students must describe their picture without looking at the others' to decide on the correct order (more challenging). This generates a lot of speaking practice and questioning.

3 Students have a picture missing and predict how the tale will end or what happened in the middle (missing picture).

4 Students listen to or read and re-order the pictures to follow the story. They then try to retell it.

5 Students complete the missing words in the speech bubbles of a cartoon story (some bits missing or last exchange). They act out the cartoon story. They could then act out a similar situation.

6 Students match words to the pictures and make sentences.

Using two contrasting photos, pictures or postcards

Suitable types are two children (one developing world/one Western European), two places (rural/urban/hot/cold), two photos of a town taken many years apart (this century/last century), two offices (hi-tech/last century), two styles of teenage room, two works of art on the same theme, two postcards of the same place, two Christmas cards, two advertisements for the same type of product, two photos of famous people with something in common.

Exploiting the contrast can give students practice in switching and contrasting tenses and using the language of comparison and speculation.

Different task types (to be used in varying combinations)

1 *'Think of adjectives to describe each photo.'*

Fig. 5 **Contrasting photos**

2 *'Describe four differences between each photo.'*

3 *'Say which photo you prefer and why'.*
'Which is the most effective advertisement?'
'Which place would you rather visit?'

Building a picture collection pp 128–9

77

4 'When do you think the photos were taken?'
'When do you think the paintings were painted?'
'What makes you think that?'

5 'Give each photo a title, or write a newspaper headline for an article which uses both photos.'

6 Use the photos to widen the discussion.
'What improvements can you see in the town?'
'What do these pictures show of changes in office work?'
'How different is life in the developing world compared to your life?'
'What aspects of Christmas do these cards emphasise?'
'Is it too commercialised?'

Magazines and brochures

Apart from providing you with plenty of images to make into flashcards and small cards, magazines are full of advertisements which can be used in contrast with each other.

Examples could be: four or five advertisements for perfume, jeans, teenage accessories or holidays; two photos to exploit (can be fashion make-overs); two teenage rooms and two lifestyles.

Mind maps

These can be built up with students:

• to brainstorm a lexical field before reading a text for discussion or listening to a song, watching a video, etc.

Example: Before reading a text on the increasing risks and dangers of sun worshipping, students are asked to work in pairs to find any words they associate with sunbathing. When these ideas are pooled on the board a mind map develops which explores ideas and provides necessary vocabulary to prepare students for the activity.

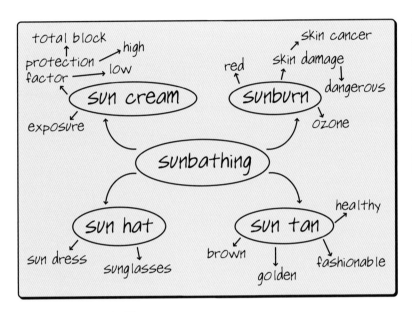

Fig. 6 **Mind map – sunbathing**

- to be used to elicit connections between ideas and events

  Example: Before reading a text on life in the Civil Rights era for young black Americans, the teacher and class develop a map relating to the era. *'Which events and people do you associate with Dr Martin Luther King?'*

- to be used in a subsequent pair or group task as lexical support to help the students find the words they need.

Unit 8 Listening and speaking

**Getting used to an
English-only classroom**
p 16

Listening skills

We learn a language through listening. Hearing your voice will be important for students. Don't feel tempted to slip into the students' language when they are struggling to understand you. This struggle is part of learning and they need time and help to tune in to you. Your main advantage is your role as a listening and speech model for students. We need to make them want to listen. But how?

From listening to speaking

Listening and speaking are usually practised together. The two levels of listening we need to focus on are:

Reading for gist
pp 114–15

Listening for gist (to get the general idea or meaning)

This means ignoring the detail and just following the overall topic even if you do not understand every word.

Reading intensively
pp 114–15

Listening for detail (to get the specific facts)

This means selectively extracting information to suit our purpose.

Example: A recorded message at an airline will give information for all customers and situations, but we may only need opening times of the sales office so we listen for that.

There are specific tasks which train students in these types of listening skills and you need to decide what your aim is for each listening you use. Some tapes, songs and videos will be listened to numerous times until students are satisfied they have extracted what they need. The first listening is usually to get the gist and then we can listen for specific detail.

A good sequence for listening could be:

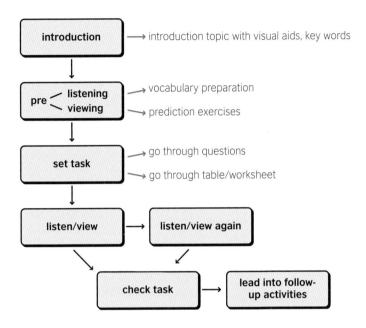

Fig. 1 **Listening procedure for tapes, songs and video**

Getting the listening level right

- It is too easy if students can get all the answers straight away on first listening. Part of training the ear is the effort and concentration required to make sense of the stream of speech.

- Give the questions before they listen so they have a reason to listen for something. Otherwise they will listen without focus, thinking they have to understand everything and feeling demotivated.

- Don't accept the right answer from the strongest student and then go on to the next question. You will be in danger of leading the level with the strongest and losing the rest. Ask for suggested answers from everyone without indicating which ones are correct at this stage. Let them listen and check.

- Encourage pair-checking and try to pair weaker students with stronger so they help each other. This is especially useful in mixed groups where you could create strong divisions between those who have finished and those who are lost.

Classroom management
pp 17–23

Dealing with mixed ability
p 19

81

- Make it clear that they do not have to understand everything to get the information they need. Telling teenagers this will have no effect. Showing them, by providing a task they can complete, makes the point.

Authentic listening versus graded listening

Authentic articles versus graded materials
p 114

In real-life listening there is a great deal of background noise. You really have to concentrate. Be aware of the acoustics in your classroom and of the quality of your machine. Test it before the lesson and find the right place on the tape if you're using a cassette. In real-life listening there is a great deal of redundancy – false starts, hesitations, repeating what you have said and verbal signals to the person speaking, e.g. *'mm ... yes ... er ... um ... yes ... that's right ... went ... went out.'* At first this can be distracting for some students.

Awareness of the stress system and linkage of sounds
pp 61–3

If we use only graded listening students do not become accustomed to the features of normal speech. Some of your classes may not have had a great deal of listening training so you need to proceed gently and prepare tasks they can achieve. Once you show (not tell) students that they do not need to understand every word then they grow in confidence and accept more authentic material.

Preparing for listening

Discussion from texts
pp 46–55

The points made for preparing a reading text for discussion and for preparing an article for class use apply to listening, and similar tasks can be used. Anticipate the subject matter, without giving all the answers away and without revealing what the listening is about. Give a reason to listen, with a short task to use during the first listening. This task should be extensive, only getting the gist and general shape of the text, e.g. *'Who is speaking?' 'Where are they?' 'What is the main topic?'*

Adapting listening up or down a level

Dealing with large classes of mixed-ability groups
p 19

- Grade the task, not the tape.

- Split the tape into shorter sections and listen a section at a time. Cut down length if necessary.

- Allow students to listen to it as many times as they need.

- Give students a say in how much to listen to or when to pause.

- Encourage plenty of checking with each other between listening.

- Anticipate the ideas or vocabulary in a pre-listening task which suits the level.

- If it becomes clear they cannot deal with the comprehension details focus on just recognising key words and the main topics. Be flexible and don't plough on if your plan has proved to be too ambitious.

Example: two tasks from the same authentic tape-recording

Use a recording of teenagers making arrangements with friends on their mobiles. It can be used with a wide range of levels. A lower level class will not be able to answer detailed comprehension questions but you can motivate them with a task to get the gist and pick out key details.

**Dealing with
the unexpected**
p 18

Task 1 – lower-intermediate (students unable to answer detailed comprehension questions)

a *What do you use your mobile for? Any other uses? Discussing homework? Telling your parents when you'll be home/arriving? Talking to your girlfriend/boyfriend? Organising your social life?*

b *Listen to these teenagers from a London secondary school.
Who is talking about ...? Number each topic: weekend activities ...
homework ... after-school activities ...*

Task 2 – upper-intermediate/advanced (students able to provide more vocabulary and analyse conversations)

a *Make a list in pairs of all the possible uses for a mobile phone for teenagers, e.g. for calling parents when you miss the bus ...*

b *Listen to these teenagers from a London secondary school.
Make notes for each conversation. Decide who is speaking: boyfriend/ girlfriend? friends? student/parent?
The reason for the call: to organise something? to talk about something?*

c *Listen again and answer 'True' or 'False' to these statements:
Douglas hasn't done his maths homework yet. True/False
Carly will probably not go out with Keith again. True/False*

Dictation

The assistant as
speech model
pp 56–7

Filler activities
p 18

Not all assistants have got a decent tape recorder or CD player, and recordings might be in short supply too. Capitalise on your voice and use it with creativity. Continental schools still make use of dictation for English teaching but you can develop this tradition by using dictogloss at all levels. (This is a technique where a text is read twice at normal speed and the students write down key words or phrases, after which they reconstruct the text together in small groups.) It is particularly useful for large classes, for groups of mixed ability and it can be a calming activity with boisterous groups. Finally, it is a great filler activity for when the tape recorder or video breaks down or your photocopies are not delivered in time.

Selective listening for text reconstruction (all levels)

Information gap
p 40

Dialogues and stories work well. Choose a short biography of a film star, pop star or international figure. Ask one half of the class to write down any key details like names, dates or major events in the person's life. Ask the other half to write only the main verbs they hear. After listening, pair students in order to pool their information. Students can ask the rest of the class questions to complete any missing detail *'Did he train in New York or LA?' 'We're not sure'.* Let the whole class pool ideas; try not to intervene. Read aloud or listen again (or watch if it is a video) to confirm that everything is understood. They can ask you to stop, repeat a bit or go on. Students will not all end up with the same text. (Note that this technique can be used with short articles from newspapers or magazines with students reading once then pooling ideas to recreate the article, not word for word.)

Revision dictation (all levels)

Encouraging
self-correction
p 31

Making revision fun
pp 99–101

Choose between five and ten questions or sentences containing language recently studied by your classes. Dictate these. Pairs check or small groups work together. Allow them to ask you to repeat specific sentences as part of their group checking. Read through once more for everyone. Students get points for each correct spelling and/or complete sentence. Vary it with one student being the writer and the other student just listening and helping the writer at each checking phase. When students control the pace of the dictation and are allowed to clear up problems they get a lot of practice in using useful language like: *'Can you say that again?' 'Sorry … I didn't hear the verb.' 'Can you say that name again?' 'Can you speak more slowly/loudly/clearly?'*

Using songs

All former assistants agree that among their most successful teaching tools are songs. Students who are usually quiet become talkative. It disguises work for the work-shy class and is a great motivator. The main pitfall is under-exploitation of the song. You can go in, play the song, give out the words and sing it. That will not fill up your fifty minutes and does not make the song a dynamic learning tool! It is also a mistake to relegate songs to the Friday afternoon or end of term treat slot. Used well, songs can be a staple part of your teaching repertoire. Songs can be used at any stage in a lesson. Just think of the song as a text or poem set to music and apply the teaching techniques for poetry and listening or reading texts for your song.

Some course books have songs especially written for EFL and there are resource materials with tailor-made songs to fit a structure. Some are good, but some are painful to listen to and don't fool teenagers. Choose wisely. Repetition is a good ingredient found in songs and this is useful for learners at all levels.

Preparing the song

Use the song title, key words, pictures and photos in the same way as when preparing reading texts or listening.

Example: John Lennon's *Imagine*
dreamer; *heaven*; *country*; *world*; *people*; *live*; *religion*; *die*
'Is this a happy or sad song?' 'Is it funny or serious?'

A sequence of drawings to illustrate the song can be used for speculation. On listening to the song they can then be put in order. If you have the music without lyrics or can play a guitar, let them hear the tune beforehand. What type of song might it be? romantic? sad? funny? What type of music is it? fast? slow? funky? jazzy? etc.

Focus on vocabulary items

- Listen and order the words as you hear them.

- Fill in the missing words and check with the song.

- Listen. How many times did you hear this word?

Motivating teenagers
pp 24–5

**Prediction techniques
for reading**
p 51

- Spot the difference. Change some words for similar-sounding ones or ones which make sense grammatically but do not make sense in the song. Students read the lyrics and try to spot the strange words. Then listen to the song and correct the different words.

Focus on structure or meaning

- Split sentences from the song into two halves and students have to match them before and during listening, e.g. linking cause and effect. You can give one half and ask them to finish *'You went away and ...'*

- Ask students to order parts of the song as they hear them. Put lines on slips of paper to re-order before and during listening.

- Blank out key verbs and students predict/match them
  'Every breath you ...   (do; take; give; break; take; make)
  Every move you ...
  Every bond you ...
  Every step you ...
  I'll be watching you'

  (*Every Breath You Take* by Sting.)

Note: Using blanks. Try to leave three or four lines clear at the beginning to get students used to the song. Put your blanks in the middle or at the end of lines. Reduce blanks to reduce the challenge if it is too difficult. Listen and do it yourself. Is there enough time between blanks to listen and write? Take the task down a level by providing a choice of two words to choose from to fill the blank space. One word might be right or both might make sense but only one is heard.

Ear training
pp 58–9

'I ... for the bus dear   (wait/run)
While riding I think of us, dear
I say a little prayer for ...'   (you/me)

(*I Say a Little Prayer* by Burt Bacharach and Hal David.)

Focus on stress and rhythm

Songs can sensitise students to stress and mouth movements. Clap or tap along with the song. This helps students get into the rhythm. Students mark the words they think will be stressed and clap on them or tap the desks or stamp their feet. (Be careful of classes above and below.) Say the song in rhythm without music, whisper it, increase the volume. Mouth the song along with the music but don't say the words out loud, just exaggerate your mouth movements and students can do the same (it's less threatening to look English than to sound English!) Always speak the song before attempting to sing it. Students who don't want to sing can mime.

Awareness of stress
pp 61–2

Focus on pronunciation

- Take out one half of a rhyme and ask students to put them back and then listen to check.

Minimal pairs
p 58

- Take out all words with the same consonant cluster or confusing vowel sounds and ask students to match them.

- Take a song with distinct rhymes and give it to students as a written text with no punctuation. It must look like a paragraph. Don't tell students that it is a song. Students punctuate the paragraph and find the rhymes. Then play the song (the surprise makes it more interesting) and get them to check and write out the lyrics. This also generates a good deal of speaking practice and thought about sentence structure and meaning.

Example: *Twenty Flight Rock*

'Well I've got a girl with a record machine when it comes to dancing she's the queen we go to dance on a Saturday night I'm all alone and I hold her tight but she lives on the twentieth floor in town and the elevator's broken down so I walk up two flights three flights four five six seven eight flights more up on the twelfth I'm starting to drag fifteenth floor and I'm ready to sag get to the top I'm too tired to rock.'

(*Twenty Flight Rock* by Ned Fairchild and Eddie Cochran)

Focus on discussing lyrics

Song lyrics can be open to a large number of possible interpretations and this ambiguity can lead to fruitful discussions. These types of song lend themselves well to speculation when people or places are not clear. Songs might refer to 'you' or 'I' or 'us' or 'them' without the listener being clear of the identity.

Example: *My Generation* by Pete Townshend
'Well, people try to put us down (Talkin' bout my generation)
Just because we get around (Talkin' bout my generation)
The things they do look awful cold (Talkin' bout my generation)
I hope I die before I get old (Talkin' bout my generation) ...' etc.

- Listen/read and say who the singers are talking about.
  Younger people/older people/people the same age

- Who do '*they*' and '*we*' refer to?

- Do you think the singers have a positive or a negative attitude towards the older generation? Why?

- Do young people in your country have a positive attitude to the older generation now?

Task (reduced form) from Exploring the English-Speaking World
by Clare Lavery

Role play and songs

After listening to the song *She's leaving home* by Lennon and McCartney, ask the students to play the roles.

Example: Student A is the girl who has left home. She has to ring home after a week to reassure her parents. Student B is an angry and worried parent who wants to persuade her to come home.

Using video

Pop videos have all the advantages of songs with the added asset of visual clues. Exploit the video with the sound off to encourage guessing about the song's meaning. Give out the lyrics (with blanks or other tasks) and continue with the sound off, using the pictures for prediction if suitable. Then listen with no picture to the music. Finally combine picture, sound and written lyrics. Experiment with different combinations of these tasks depending on the song and the usefulness of the video.

Example: Half the students see the video with no sound and take notes on what they think the song is about while the other half are given the lyrics to re-order in another place so they don't see the video. Combine students from each group to pool their resources.

The potential and the pitfalls

The principles of listening skills apply to video. However, you also have the help of visual clues (place, facial expression and gesture) to aid your understanding. We need to train students to make use of these clues to arrive at meaning. This means that previewing tasks and initial viewing tasks need to focus on questions about the people and their attitude or relationship to each other. Doing this first viewing with the sound off focuses students on this vital aspect. There are many excellent videos made especially for ELT and some textbooks have accompanying videos. However, if your school doesn't have this expensive material you can use your own, but you need to prepare it well.

Parallel sources of meaning
p 68

Intonation practice
pp 63–4

Tips and solutions

- **Active viewing**. Watching the television is a passive activity at home but in the language classroom it needs to be an active experience for students to learn. Don't just switch on and sit back for forty-five minutes. You need the help of tasks and a clear plan to get students involved and really listening.

- **Short sequences**. Use no more than one- to three-minute sequences, since you will be rewinding, reviewing and doing two or or three tasks with the material. That's sufficient for fifty minutes of class time.

- **Don't have the television on all the time**. Switch off completely when students are working on their tasks. It's a big distraction to have a fuzzy screen in the corner. If students don't have a break between each viewing they will suffer overload and switch off. Take it slowly, in clear steps.

Using off-air video

Creating meaningful information gaps p 40

Authentic versus graded listening pp 81–2

Break down your sequences into sections of a minute or so, but use maximum three to four minutes for a fifty-minute lesson. Use a recognition task with lower levels but more detailed comprehension and vocabulary tasks with more advanced students. Adapt approaches to suit your students' level and needs.

Example: Using advertisements. This always works well with students but select carefully as sense of humour changes from culture to culture and references to topical things might confuse.

- Students hear advertisement but don't watch it. Using the main words, try to predict the product, then view.

- Some students watch with no sound and describe what is happening to others not watching.

- Students imagine what is being said and write a script, then compare to the real version.

Role play from cartoons, dialogues and video clips

A good introduction to role play is to see a similar situation in action. A funny situation in a strip cartoon, a short clip from a video or even a clip from a comedy programme can inspire parallel situations. After reading or seeing the model, encourage suggestions of parallel situations from students and alternative vocabulary.

Recording or filming role plays

Some students really enjoy recording themselves, playing it back and then trying again. This encourages a great deal of self-correction and you can exploit these moments to focus on improving intonation and pronunciation. This can take time, even over two lessons with good groups, but it is highly motivating.

Controlled dialogue practice p 39

Learners' sense of progress p 29

Unit 9 Games

Games in the language classroom

Motivating learners
pp 24–5

- **Help to involve learners actively** in the learning process.

- **Provide a challenge** which encourages learners to stretch themselves (in order to win). Most games involve learners in reactivating the language they have studied and in trying to use it meaningfully.

- **Help learners to forget they are studying**: they lose themselves in the fun of the game and the activity motivates them.

Dealing with
mixed-ability groups
p 19

- **Encourage collaborative learning**. Team games require pooling of knowledge, pair games require co-operation and turn-taking. Students can learn from one another. A good reader with a more proficient speaker can combine skills to make a winning team.

- **Provide variety of pace**. Games can be short, long and can involve writing, speaking, listening or reading. They are excellent for motivating pupils whose attention is wandering, filling a dull Friday afternoon lesson, revising in a fun way, saving the day when the video machine breaks down or when the reading you wanted to do has gone down like a lead balloon.

Making repetition fun
pp 60–1

- **Give extra practice without inducing boredom**. Many games involve repetition of the same language over and over again. In normal circumstances this would feel artificial and be demotivating.

Management of games

- **The rules have to be as clear as possible**. Complicated scoring and long lists of rules can draw the focus of the lesson away from using language. Stick to basic card games, keep to one topic for a game or try and adapt local games to which everyone knows the rules.

- **Don't explain the game – demonstrate it**. Always have a trial run before starting the game proper and you play a team member in the rehearsal.

- **Don't let games drag on too long**. Set time limits for answering questions (e.g. a buzzer, a bell, a whistle or a slow count down from five when time is up – these theatrical bits also make the game fun for all learners).

- **Try to use games where there is more than one winner**. Everyone then feels they stand a chance of winning and is more willing to try. Games must seem achievable in order to appeal to learners.

- **Assess the learning value of a game**. Some games might be fun to play but are all the students involved? Are they all using language or hearing language again?

- **Consider very carefully the language needed** to play the game. What will the students have to say to each other to guess a person's card? Try the game with a friend or play it through in your head. Does it activate the language you want to practise? Have students got the necessary vocabulary to play it successfully?

- **Balance the types of games you use**. Vary whole class games with card games in pairs, noisy team games, and quiet concentration games for calming down an over-excited class.

- **Don't overuse games**. Games are a motivator but lose their challenge and interest if they become an everyday routine. They need to be seen as a special moment.

Setting up pair work
p 20

Pace in classroom
management
p 17

Using the learner's
own culture
p 110

Working
with teachers
pp 5–7

Revision games
p 99

Tips for creating games to suit your classes

- **Personalise or localise games**. A game or quiz about famous people can include not only internationally known stars but local people too. Use television, teenage and local celebrity magazines. Mix pictures of local television, sports and music personalities or political and controversial figures with more widely known faces. Students find these quizzes more challenging as not all of them, for example, would recognise the country's football captain or an important politician. The information gap is genuine and meaningful. Stick mixed groups of personalities on A4-sized sheets and photocopy them if you can. Students in small groups or pairs can then have a number of sheets to work from when challenging each other.

- **Adapt games to suit all levels if possible** (to make the most of the material you have prepared). The Famous Person game can work with beginners asking: *'Is he Italian?' 'Is he French?' 'Where's he/she from?'* and can work equally well with advanced students who can invent complex clues or questions to guess the personality, e.g. *'He's well known in this country for his music but he comes from America and sings in a boy band. Who is he?'*

- **Invent games which recycle language from the main textbook**. If you note that learners have covered time-telling this week in their main lessons with their teacher, you can prepare a short time bingo game with blank clock faces on cards. Each pupil fills in the clock faces and then the teacher calls out a random time, picks clock faces from a hat or says sentences including the times.

Types of games

Card games

Start with a set of flashcards. Elicit the words for each card then choose a card and ask students to find out which card you have by questioning you. Direct the questioning with examples of the types of question you would like to be asked, if specific structures are to be used. If the activity is to focus less on accuracy and more on fluency, allow students more freedom to experiment with question types. Obviously the less-guided approach suits intermediate learners upwards. A lower-level group will need question prompts on the board to help them.

Example: Holiday destinations game
Using a set of large glossy pictures of different holiday locations from brochures and small packs of six to eight cards of similar pictures cut from holiday brochures. The locations could be in English-speaking countries, e.g. the Australian Outback, Cape Town, Alaska.

- Show the large pictures at great speed and students guess what they can see. *'Is it a ...?'*

- Show four or five pictures and then cover them. Choose one of them, and have the students ask questions to guess which one you have chosen, e.g. *'I went on holiday to this place.'* (The teacher has chosen a picture of African safari from a collection of photos of holiday places from travel brochures.) Students ask: *'Was it a hot country?'* *'Were there any beaches?'* *'Did you see any animals?'*

Dialogue games with card prompts
After practising a dialogue with flashcards of say, drinks, with the whole class, put students in pairs with a pack of cards (drinks, food, snacks) to challenge each other. Student A picks up a card and offers a drink. Student B responds refusing the drink, and Student A offers an alternative by picking up another card. One point is gained if each student is able to use the appropriate word correctly. Students keep the card if they manage to say something about it which is appropriate. You can use mixed cards of this type for revision as long as the person who picks up a card can ask an appropriate question with it. This is a motivating game for younger and lower-level students as the cards give reassurance as well as reminding them of the vocabulary.

Using flashcards
p 73

Sources of pictures
pp 128–9

Speech work
pp 56–67

Meaningful dialogue practice with picture prompts
p 39

Sources of games
pp 129–130, 135–6

Memory games

Even commercially produced games which you have at home can be used for language practice. Memory games are essentially sets of pairs of pictures but you can also add matching cards with words for each picture. They are popular games with primary and secondary learners in Europe. Look out for local card games which can be used: the staff at school might be able to help.

Bingo

Prepare blank cards containing eight boxes and keep a good number of them for moments when you need a filler activity. Write twenty words on the board. (You control the language of the game.) Ask students to choose eight of the words and write them in the boxes on their cards or draw pictures of the words with younger learners. The most basic method is then to call out words, but this can be more challenging and varied if you call out sentences or clues for the word. For example, instead of calling out the word *'car'* you can say *'Far too many people use these to travel short distances instead of using public transport. They are making pollution in cities worse.'*

Picture pairs/snap/happy families

Many assistants find these games are useful as they can be good for reactivating language and giving practice in questioning.

Games for asking questions

Using pictures to spot the difference
pp 75–6

A lot of the games outlined in this unit involve students in asking questions. To be an active participant in a two-way conversation it is important to be able to show interest and find out information by responding to people and asking questions. Too often in large classes in state schools in Continental Europe the students get little practice in asking questions. This can be a real weakness. They might answer plenty of the teacher's questions but not find themselves in meaningful situations where questions are needed for true communication to occur. Start with: *'Find someone who ...'*

Controlled speaking activities
p 37

Questions are also needed when you meet other people speaking English (native or non-native) to clarify meaning or misunderstanding. Students really need to practise asking about unknown words. Start with: *'What do you mean ...?'*

Games which focus on defining objects or words can be a useful way of practising questions, e.g. *'Guess my object: is it animal, vegetable or mineral?'*

Call my bluff is a good example of a definitions game which can be used, in a less sophisticated way, in language classes. Prepare one word and give the students three possible definitions for it. Ask them to guess the correct definition. This game also encourages students to make logical, intelligent guesses at the meaning of unknown words. With more advanced learners you can give them words and a dictionary and they invent three definitions, one true and the other two false.

Games for fluency

These games do not just focus on using the right vocabulary or structures but encourage learners to use all the language at their disposal to communicate freely.

Just a minute

Based on the BBC Radio 4 programme, this game can be used with any topic. It works best with advanced students. A student in each team must talk for one minute without: a) repeating words, b) straying from the topic, c) hesitating. Award points for each person who manages to speak for a minute. Use it for revision by choosing topic areas recently covered in the main syllabus or issues discussed recently.

Dilemmas/Scruples/Taboo-type games

This type of game has proved popular with sixteen-year-olds upwards. Students have packs of cards on which a series of hypothetical questions are written, e.g. *'If you could go back in time, when would you go back to?' 'Why?' 'What would you do if ... ?'* (Embarrassing situations/getting yourself out of a fix.) Other contestants can ask difficult questions if you want to make these games more challenging.

The scoring in these games depends on how well the challenged student defends his or her choice of action. A panel of students awards points from one to five (holding up score cards like in a television quiz game).

Using information gap activities for communication
p 40

Vocabulary games
p 98

Controlled versus free practice
pp 36–45

Using photographs
pp 77–8

Describing photographs

Students are given unusual, striking photographs and have to say as much as they can about them without repeating themselves. It can be done in a large class with photographs circulating around the room. This is a useful activity in education systems where photo descriptions and discussion based on a photo form an integral part of the oral exams in schools.

'I have used a word game with all my classes and it worked. I wrote some words down and asked each pupil to take a word on a piece of paper. The pupils then had to explain what the word was so that their neighbour could guess what they were talking about. It really made the pupils start talking'.
Liz Hall, Flensburg, Germany. Assistant in a Gymnasium.

Vocabulary games

Dealing with the unexpected
p 18

These can be played with the whole class or in pairs or teams/groups. They make excellent fillers for the end of lessons, warm-ups to prepare a topic area and life-savers when you stand in for a colleague at short notice. The best games need only a piece of chalk and a board.

Hangman

Limit the topic area, e.g. animals or verbs of sense or emotion. It is a good game for getting students in large traditional classes used to participating. First run the game yourself, then involve students in coming to the board and running the game, then play it in teams and then in small groups or pairs. Another popular version is shark spelling. Draw a sea and enormous shark with wide open mouth at the bottom of the board. Draw a stick man at the top of the board. With each wrong guess the stick man moves closer to the shark's mouth until he is eaten. Expand this game to use names of people, song titles, book or film titles.

Writing slowly on the board

Put up the first consonant of a word. Can students guess what word it is? Gradually add consonants. For team playing, get the teams to draw up their words before the contest begins. Use the OHP (overhead projector) or computer projector to show distorted words for guessing (upside down, out of focus, the top or bottom half of the word).

Charades

Use pictures or words on pieces of paper in a hat or box. Divide class into teams (three teams in large class). Each team takes turns to pull out a challenge from the hat and mime the word for his team-members to guess. This can be done with all action adverbs, such as angrily, happily, quickly.

Categorisation

Give students a list of words (no more than twenty-five or thirty). These can be from recent reading texts, from recent work covered with their teacher or simply vocabulary areas you would like to focus on. Students can work individually, in pairs or small groups. Divide the words into categories and give each category a name.

Revision games (or recycling textbook work in a fun way!)

Many assistants are asked to revise language, especially as the school year progresses. They have commented that they also start running out of ideas or get fed up with playing the same games. Fortunately some of the most successful revision games are those generated by students themselves. In these games the students suggest the language, not the teacher.

Board games

Make a standard route, like a long snake with start to finish, or a snakes and ladders type board. An A4 sheet size is sufficient. Leave squares blank and have a blank photocopy to complete with challenges. Choose the language you wish to revise and put instructions in each square. Even beginners can play this!

Using errors
to give a sense
of progress
p 29

Example:
'Have you ever been on a plane?' (Yes ... move two spaces)
'Describe what you do on Saturday afternoons.' (move three spaces)
'Spell your address.' (move three spaces)

With more advanced learners the challenges can be more open-ended, encouraging fluency. Example: *'Describe your plans for when you leave school next year.'*

Student-generated board games work well too. Students in pairs make challenges on a blank photocopied board. Then the board is passed around so a different pair plays with it. This is best if they have played before and you direct them to topic/conversation areas based on recent work in the textbook.

Revision bubbles

Revision bubbles are a good way of doing student-generated revision of structures and vocabulary. This game can be played with students after only a few lessons of English – or many years. Draw a bubble on the board and ask for suggestions from the class to fill the bubble, e.g. any words from the previous month's work. You can specify the types of words that you want the students to give (e.g. verbs, pronouns, adjectives).

Encouraging peer correction through group work
p 31

- Students in pairs or small groups make as many sentences or questions possible using their words. Set a time limit of ten minutes. Give one point for each correct sentence.

- Students have ten to fifteen minutes to write a short dialogue incorporating as many of their words as possible, and they then act out the dialogues.

- Students categorise their words, inventing any categories they wish (including grammatical categories).

Dealing with large classes of mixed ability
p 19

Students develop technique as they play these games. They soon realise that if a dialogue is required they are wise to include useful verbs and they start to suggest high value items for their bubbles.

Using cross-curicular content
pp 108–9

Question challenge based on the textbook

Each student prepares two or three questions based on the last five units or so in their textbook. Put students in pairs or small groups next lesson to pool their questions. Then they challenge another team to answer the question. One point for correct answer, half a point for comprehensible but inaccurate answer. This game works with eleven-year-olds after just one term of English and eighteen-year-olds of upper-intermediate level because it is the students themselves who control the language of the game. You can direct the quizzes by giving categories, such as food, geography, school, etc.

Example: Student questions for the category 'Geography' in a college.
'Is Turkey in the EU?'
'Where is the singer Dido from?'
'What is the population of France?'
'What colours are in the Italian flag?'

Students become very inventive when planning these quizzes and get great satisfaction if they can bring in knowledge from other areas of their school curriculum, such as maths or science. Students who say English is not their favourite of subjects become motivated enough to talk about a subject they enjoy in school.

Spot the nonsense

Prepare ten or so sentences based on recent language areas covered then mix up words from these sentences. Each sentence contains a word which has jumped from another. The first pair to sort out the nonsense and make each sentence make sense are the winners. This can be done with letters, postcards or short texts too, or a postcard written from holiday using all the opposites which have to be changed. Example: *'It's lovely and rainy and we're having an awful time'. 'When we got up last night the sky was a beautiful shade of blue.'*

Instead of wrong words put jumbled letters so they have to guess the word from context and unscramble it.

Nonsense dialogues are enjoyed too. Mix up two or three short conversations (even from textbooks). Small groups unscramble them, then act them out.

Motivating teenagers
pp 24–5

Self-correction
p 31

Unit 10 Cultural content

The assistant as cultural resource

**Working with
teachers**
pp 5–9

Most assistants find that students are very interested in their lives and in their country. In some cases you may be the first and only person from the UK they have ever met. The countries described in their books and on television will suddenly come to life with you. It is only natural for them to try out all their misconceptions, making assumptions about you as if you were a stereotyped English person who drinks tea and loves the Royal Family – no matter if you are of Irish or Asian descent and have never watched a game of cricket! Your patience will be tested to the limit with generalisations about your country and questions about your values and attitudes. It is only natural for students to glean what they can from family, friends and media. You may find a student whose knowledge is based on an uncle's two-month stay back in 1955 or a teacher who had a year abroad in the 1970s. Your own experience of the UK is your main asset for teachers and students to tap in to. You can use this knowledge to the benefit of learners by following some simple guidelines:

**Teacher
talking time**
p 36

• Distinguish between personal experience and national experience. Your own region and family life are one example of many different lifestyles in the UK. Talk about your experience with enthusiasm but make it clear that this is not representative of all UK people and habits.

• Avoid generalisations beginning with: *'British people think that ...'* It is wiser to qualify statements with *'There is a tendency to think ...'* or *'some sections of the population believe ...'* Try to avoid creating stereotypes about your own culture.

• Students may happily listen to your account of yourself and country for hours but you need to structure this learning to suit the language classroom. This means less teacher talking time and more student involvement in the process. (See below.) There is a danger of giving lectures.

• Use this work in cultural studies to find out more about the host culture. Show students that you also value their world and experience and encourage contributions to your cultural topics.

What is culture?

It is too simplistic to view culture as a list of facts that we associate with
a society, for example, that Britain is an island and that Australians like barbecues.
Apart from creating stereotypes we risk a 'trivial pursuit' approach to culture. It is
true that members of a given society share a body of knowledge which could be
termed common culture or shared culture. This could be anything from knowing
the name of a television programme from the 1970s or the symbol of a political
party. In essence, it is the *Who wants to be a millionaire?* knowledge which comes
from living there and going through the education system. It would be difficult to
transmit a fraction of this knowledge to a foreign learner. It is possible however
to identify commonly shared values and trends in the English-speaking world.
These factors determine the social and economic fabric of everyday life and
can be used as the basis for cultural studies in a language classroom. Instead
of simply looking at a who's who? of the Royal Family, the approach can, by
comparison, be far less superficial by looking at how the Royal Family are viewed
in the UK today and what their role was in the past. It is important to transmit the
concept that societies, like your and the students' own, are not static. Behaviour,
habits and attitudes have evolved and are constantly changing. Stereotypes
of yesteryear are no longer valid. One major theme, for upper secondary in
particular, is the impact that the Information Revolution is having on working
patterns, life styles and ways of learning, free time and communicating.

**Choosing
suitable content**
p 47

What types of material can be used to introduce a cultural topic?

Realia

Money, stamps, menus, maps, greetings cards, packets from products, leaflets, etc.

Example: A real Christmas pudding (even if uncooked in its box – hygiene laws
might prevent you taking real cooked recipes into schools). Ask students to guess
the ingredients and feel the weight.

Using visual aids
pp 68–79

Example: A selection of greetings cards (including cyber cards you can send free to yourself as examples), which you can display on walls or a large desk. Using your cards, students make a list of celebrations and occasions for card-giving. Do they send cards for these occasions? This can be good lead-in to the topic of local or national customs. These cards can also reflect the racial and cultural diversity of the UK.

Photos, posters, postcards and drawings

Contrasting photos
pp 77–8

Combinations can reflect the rural-versus-urban environment or lifestyles, ethnic communities, diversity of housing and interiors of homes, different types of classrooms, types of jobs or roles of men and women.

Example: A selection of food and drink pictures from magazines can lead in to the topic of multicultural Britain and changing eating patterns. Students divide their food pictures into categories: snacks, possible breakfast foods, foods most likely to be on a canteen menu, etc. They get some real surprises by doing this and it challenges their assumptions.

Questionnaires and surveys

**Using questionnaires
for discussion**
p 41

An alternative way of giving information at a lower level to avoid dense texts. The results of national surveys can be looked at to introduce issues.

Example: A national survey published people's attitudes to their own country with questions like 'What makes you most proud when you think of the UK?' or 'What makes you most embarrassed when you think of the UK?'

Graphs, tables, diagrams, maps and statistics

These can be interpreted without too much language. Students tick the sentences which best match the information in the graphs.

Quizzes based on a map can help students learn about the UK, or can review the language of geography.

Voxpops from magazines or papers

Voxpops are where several people are surveyed in the street for their opinion on an issue. Similar collections of opinions can be used from discussion groups on the Internet (especially on issues in the news).

Example: *Do you think gun control laws are strict enough?* from US teen website after high school shootings. Two or three readers' letters from the national press or teen magazines can be used in a similar way, balancing for and against or reflecting the diversity of debate within the nation.

Songs, music, rhymes, poetry and literature

These can all introduce social contexts, geographical areas and periods in history. Combinations of these can build up a rich tapestry on a theme.

Video and off-air television

These reflect lifestyles and habits, not just tourist information programmes.

What is cultural competence?

Many people living and working abroad have commented that they feel closer to understanding their own culture through living abroad. This is mainly because the experience of adapting to a new country forces us into considering our own lifestyle and values. Everyone thinks that their way is the norm, but this is clearly not the case. Cultural competence involves accepting that there are many different ways of living, thinking, worshipping and behaving. The reading and discussion tasks given to students should require them to make comparisons with their own country and cultural values. This mimics the process of cross cultural development. A lesson where the assistant just talks about the UK and students ask questions about the UK is clearly not the solution. Tasks given to students must require them to bring their own experience to bear on the topic. This can be done with very low-level learners without the need for lengthy discussions beyond students' linguistic competence.

Example: Compare the ways in which the following simple school timetable from an assistant's local secondary school in the UK has been exploited.

Using the media
pp 114–15, 123–5

Using songs and poetry
pp 85–8, 117–21

Using video
pp 89–91

Fig. 1 **Sample UK school timetable**

Day	Time	Subject	Teacher	Room
Monday	9.00–9.45 9.45–10.30	Geography Geography	Mr Stewart Mr Stewart	L11 L11
	break			
	10.45–11.30 11.30–12.15	Science Science	Mr Evans Mr Evans	S10 S10
	lunch			
	1.30–2.15 2.15–3.00 3.00–3.45	English History History	Mrs Bainbridge Miss McArthur Miss McArthur	W6 W22 W22
Tuesday	9.00–9.45 9.45–10.30	Maths set Y4 Maths set Y4	Mr Finnemore Mr Finnemore	W11 W11
	break			
	10.45–11.30 11.30–12.15	Music Music	Mr Russell Mr Russell	B2 B2
	lunch			
	1.30–2.15 2.15–3.00 3.00–3.45	French French Business Studies	Mrs Mallows Mrs Mallows Mrs Mayze	W6 W6 L3
Wednesday	9.00–9.45 9.45–10.30	Science Science	Mr Evans Mr Evans	S10 S10
	break			
	10.45–11.30 11.30–12.15	Maths set Y4 Maths set Y4	Mr Finnemore Mr Finnemore	W11 W11
	lunch			
	1.30–2.15 2.15–3.00 3.00–3.45	English Physical Education Physical Education	Mrs Bainbridge Mrs Fallon Mrs Fallon	W6 PE PE
Thursday	9.00–9.45 9.45–10.30	Design Technology Design Technology	Mr Rhodes Mr Rhodes	TECH TECH
	break			
	10.45–11.30 11.30–12.15	German German	Miss Reynolds Miss Reynolds	W24 W24
	lunch			
	1.30–2.15 2.15–3.00 3.00–3.45	Computing Studies French Science	Mr Bird Mrs Mallows Mr Evans	L2 W6 S10
Friday	9.00–9.45 9.45–10.30	History History	Miss McArthur Miss McArthur	W22 W22
	break			
	10.45–11.30 11.30–12.15	English English	Mrs Bainbridge Mrs Bainbridge	W6 W6
	lunch			
	1.30–2.15 2.15–3.00 3.00–3.45	Modern Studies Religious Studies Religious Studies	Mr Johnson Miss Reynolds Miss Reynolds	L14 W23 W23

Task one

Look at this timetable and answer in pairs:

- What time do students start school?

- Do they have a long school day?

- Which languages do they study?

- Do they have any breaks?

- Divide the subjects into arts or sciences. What other subjects are studied?

- Describe this timetable to your partner. Start: *'In the UK students go to school five days a week ...'*

Task two

Look at this timetable and answer in pairs:

- Is the school day in the UK shorter or longer than yours? Is the timetable lighter or heavier?

- Find two other differences, e.g. starting time; breaks; number of hours of sport or languages.

- Tick any subjects that you enjoy on this timetable. Is there anything new? ... or missing?

- Think of another question to ask about education in the UK.

- In pairs or groups choose two more courses that you think your school might offer to students, e.g. fashion and design or technology and music. Does anything surprise you? Say why they are useful. Plan your ideal school week and timetable.

Learner-centred tasks for revision
pp 31, 100

Learner-centred tasks for fluency practice
p 43

Learner-centred tasks for texts
pp 72, 84

Open-ended questions
pp 16–17

Task one clearly exploits the timetable but restricts itself to the UK. The questions can be answered with one word and very quickly. Students do little more than repeat information without much reflection. The final task is simply to regurgitate the information in an unrealistic mini-lecture. In *Task two* students need to think about the information and apply it to their own experience and situation. They are asked to interact and to reflect beyond the data. The timetable in *Task two* also becomes a springboard for a more controlled discussion on the types of subjects that interest young people and some initiative is given to students to

**Teaching
mixed-ability classes**
p 19

formulate further questions about the topic. Obviously you can do a great deal more with higher-level learners in upper secondary schools but *Task two* has been used very successfully with whole classes in lower secondary schools. The open-ended questioning in *Task two* also makes it more suitable for mixed-ability groups as students contribute what they can, using the language at their disposal.

Techniques for developing competence

Bring misconceptions into the open

What is the received knowledge? How far is it true? Find out what students believe to be true and compare it to reality. What do they already know?

Example: Use questionnaires as a lead-in to a topic or ask students to predict what they will be told. It doesn't matter if students cannot complete the whole questionnaire.

**Introducing topics
for speaking**
pp 46–51

The UK and devolution
Look at the map of the UK in pairs.

- Can you fill in the names of the countries: Northern Ireland/England/ Scotland/Wales?

- Put the capitals on the map: Belfast/London/Cardiff/Edinburgh.

- In which of these capital cities will you find Westminster?

- What do you call the people who come from ... England?
  (the English/English people) Scotland? Wales? Northern Ireland?

Man and the elements (the Australian Outback)
Here are some words which people associate with Australia. Do these words refer to people, places or things? Are they in your dictionary?

Outback   Aborigine   Sydney   continent   suburbs

Where do most Australians originally come from?

Which language do they speak?

Challenge stereotypes

Compare stereotyped images with realistic images. Explore notions of stereotype. What is expected of men, women, older or younger people? Focus on roles in society.

Example: Ask the following before reading an article from *The Guardian* (which interviews parents and young people about at what age they should leave home and how much young people participate in the household in the UK):

Before you read discuss in pairs:
Who does the following chores in your family? Washing clothes; cleaning; shopping for food; cooking; emptying rubbish; making beds; ironing.

Do any of these statements reflect attitudes of people in your country?
Parents should look after their kids until they're ready to leave home.
Young adults who stay at home should pay for food and bills.
Young people should get their own place once they reach eighteen.
When both parents work they should both cook, clean and shop for food.

Focus on research skills

Looking at societies as a researcher develops skills for cultural understanding. Rather than giving students the information, design lessons where they have to look for it, e.g. developing the ability to link cause and effect, to balance disadvantages and advantages or to find historic, economic or geographic reasons for habits and ways of life.

> The birth of Youth Culture
> Complete the sentences (or match two parts) using the data you have:
>
> • There were a lot of young people in the UK in 1959 because ...
>
> • Teenage culture was able to develop in the UK because ...

Data-response techniques are used extensively across the curriculum and can be seen in subject disciplines like sociology, history, geography, business studies or media studies. Cultural Studies brings in aspects from all curriculum areas, so the techniques suited to each subject can be used in the language classroom. It is also easier to answer questions on a map showing climatic difference in the UK than to answer questions based on a lengthy text which artificially gives the same information.

Personalising tasks
p 52

Resources for texts
pp 54–5

Suitable topics for different learners

Resources for Cultural Studies pp 126–9

Bearing in mind the experience and intellectual maturity of the learners, the following topics have been used in Continental European schools with success.

Younger learners

Topics should focus more on the concrete relating to lifestyle and habits. Include some making and doing activities like making an Easter or Christmas card, making posters of topics, drawing maps or pictures to illustrate topics. Try to keep to visual stimulus with the addition of story-telling, songs and rhymes.

- **Topics related to the seasonal calendar**. Christmas traditions, card-giving habits, Halloween stories and customs, Guy Fawkes story and parties, Easter, half-term holidays from school, autumn traditions, different religious festivals in the UK, etc.

- **Topics related to students' lives**. School and the school day, extra-curricular activities at school, towns, villages and cities, basic climate and geography, spare-time activities, television and media, pets, home life, eating patterns, etc.

Older teenagers/young adults

Using authentic sources of text pp 114–5

More mature teenagers are ready for more reflection. Keep to topics which they have experience of through their own lives or those of their parents, grandparents and local area. Consider topics such as: the changes in their own society; the different roles and expectations; the freedom of young people; or anything related to generations to be potentially stimulating for the students.

Using contrasting genres

Using songs pp 85–8

Combining a song with a short literary extract or some background reading or an autobiography/biography of a person can provide material for two or three lessons used to explore an era in history or a theme related to cultural identity. Song lyrics often reflect the concerns of the day and the culture of the singers and these can be exploited to introduce and discuss cultural topics. Protest songs, ballads, soul and blues are good examples of this. Introduce Black American history with some Black American music or a poem or some photos of the civil rights era. Songs add variety and make the cultural links for students.

The impact of the Internet on Cultural Studies

Internet resources
pp 133–5

Students and teachers in the past could get cultural information from television, films and library books or textbooks. The textbooks had got their information from other books on history, geography or social studies. Sometimes it was possible to set up a school exchange visit to the UK or get a class to exchange pen friend letters. Now, at the click of a mouse, you can visit any English-speaking country, make a virtual tour of a museum, read about and chat to real people. Instead of reading about the Industrial Revolution in your traditional textbook you can go into an interactive schools website and read the original first-hand interviews with young children in factories in the UK in the 1830s! History comes to life and horizons are broadened. The Internet has brought personal accounts, access to visual material and real contacts, and is changing the face of cultural studies lessons. There has never been a better time to find teaching material and to motivate language learners to appreciate cultural content.

Projects and student research

Resources for project work
pp 133–5

Projects provide creative opportunities for meaningful language use at all language levels from primary upwards. You can introduce short, controlled projects to start.

Example: Making a list of products from the English-speaking world in their supermarket or using their local press to see how many English words are used. On a larger scale, the project may be an ongoing activity involving students collecting data on American television programmes, following references in the press to events in the UK, surfing the Internet to find out about a person or an era, or making posters for their classroom. The best types of projects are those which draw on the students' own experience and world in comparison to another English-speaking country.

Unit 11 Literature and the media

Using authentic sources of text

Differences between graded language learning materials and the real thing

Using visuals
pp 68–79

- **Vocabulary load.** An average quality newspaper is written at a vocabulary level of 20,000 words, which is far beyond that of the average language learner. There are also many colloquial expressions, phrases and idioms that your learners would not find in their textbooks. Tabloids are even more difficult.

  Solution: Avoid full-page Sunday supplement-type articles, favouring short-and-to-the-point articles with visual support in photos, useful diagrams or headlines. Prepare the vocabulary background well before reading. This can be done using games and mind maps, or brainstorming using pictures or photos related to the theme. It is better if the text or poem is too easy. You can then add lots of tasks to work with it, rather than struggling and wading through a text which is just too lexically dense.

Cultural reference
pp 110–11

- **Reference.** Authentic texts may have a high proportion of reference to background information and facts that you would only know by having been brought up in the culture or being schooled in the education system. Articles, extracts and poems that are referentially dense are demotivating and unsuitable.

Articles for
teenagers
p 131

  Solution: Pick and choose very carefully while avoiding the absolutely bland. How much does the subject matter relate to students' knowledge of the world, their experiences and their concerns? Are your seventeen-year-old lycée students really as interested in a particular topic as you or their parents? Just because the media is throwing up a lot of articles it doesn't mean the topic is suitable for your conversation class.

Types of reading – intensive or extensive?

Types of
discussion tasks
pp 51–3

It is important to decide what you are going to do with a text. If it is to encourage discussion in a conversation lesson then you need to read it extensively. This means you will introduce the text, pre-read, go through comprehension of the main ideas with a task, and then go on to discussing those ideas or using them as the basis for a group speaking task. If you are reading the text for intensive purposes then you would dwell more on points of grammar and vocabulary, text structure or maybe lead into a writing activity with the text as model. Assistants are generally required to get students talking, and extensive reading of texts is a more suitable approach in most cases.

Tips for dealing with reading

- **Students may expect to understand every word** and want to work through a text word for word. Giving them a specific task avoids this as well as giving them something which is not too dense for their level. Short is best.

- **Going through every item of vocabulary and grammar** will not make them better readers and will soon remove the interest and pleasure. Try to leave the intensive work to a class teacher, unless instructed otherwise.

- **Vary the text types**. Use advertisements, brochures, reviews, brief news items, anecdotes, letters, agony columns, personal letters, very short dialogues and postcards, etc.

Authentic versus graded listening
p 82

Types of reading tasks to use for dialogues and texts

- Match illustrations to a text or complete a diagram summarising the text.

- Re-order jumbled paragraphs or jumbled sentences or questions and replies.

- Insert two or three sentences which have been taken out and need putting back.

- Complete a table of advantages/disadvantages, main points or key data.

- Give a text or dialogue with no last paragraph or no last section. Students then discuss what it might contain.

Literary extracts

Assistants asked to use literature in their classes are generally working with older, more advanced-level students. However, we cannot assume that these students are able to express their opinions on the literary texts as well as they are able to understand them. Have they had practice in talking about literature in English? Think back to your sixth-form literature classes. Did you discuss your set texts in English or in the language you were studying? It can vary but it has implications for the assistant.

Resources for literature
p 137

Liaising with teachers
pp 3–7

- Find out if there is a school policy regarding teaching approaches to literature.

- Many teachers assume you know about English literature or how to teach it. Ask for help if you need it.

- Actively seek help from colleagues, ELT resources, other assistants and the assistants' website.

- Look at resource material prepared for teaching literature to younger students in the UK.

Literary material aimed at native speakers

It is not enough to write a list of comprehension questions and walk in. You will have a very, very long fifty minutes and will end up doing a lot of the work. A non-native speaker cannot cope with the length and depth of text intended for a native speaker of the same age. Plan guided reading tasks to help them.

What if you are not asked to include literature in your teaching?

Some modern literature, especially for young adults and teenagers, can provide stimulus texts as much as a copy of a newspaper can. If teachers ask you to use a lot of articles, vary this with a short extract from fiction. You can even serialise a short teenage story or novel over an entire school term if students show enthusiasm.

Example: A very short extract from Nick Hornby's *Fever Pitch* can be used successfully. The main character describes the moment he found that he could have a relationship with his Dad by going to football together.

Extracts from books which have been made into films which students may know are usually well received. Extracts on the BBC's website for language learners will give you a good indication of types and tasks to use.

Example: Extracts from *Bridget Jones's Diary, Captain Corelli's Mandolin* or *The God of Small Things* have been used.

Try to avoid:

Teaching with cultural content
pp 110–11

- **Long extracts**. Don't use more than half a page or two short extracts from one page.

- **Too much colloquial dialogue or slang**. You will get bogged down in explanations, leaving little room for students to contribute.

- **Reference to cultural events and people unknown to students**. This would require too much background information. It's fine to give one-line explanations but if they need a mini-lecture on the period to get to grips with the extract, it is not suitable for your aims as an assistant.

Poetry

Poetry doesn't have to mean Wordsworth. Not with sixteen-year-old lower intermediate learners. However, don't exclude poetry. It can be a brilliant source of short, lively material which can bring one simple story or idea to life. Poetry doesn't have to be serious and it can be appealing to an average group of non-academic adolescents if the subject matter reflects their world and concerns. Poetry is also music, it helps students tune in to the rhythm of English, the rhymes and the sounds of the language. It lends itself to acting out, and to thought-provoking discussion. The pleasure of getting your mouth round English rhythm and sounds can appeal to teenagers. Those too embarrassed to sing will recite a poem!

Motivating teenagers
pp 24–5

Using songs
pp 85–8

Making a poetry cassette
p 126

A bad habit by Michael Rosen

'Cigarette, Mike?' they say,
'I don't smoke,' I say.
'Haven't you got any bad habits?' they say,
'Yes,' I say, 'I chew bus tickets.'
I can't stop it.
The conductor gives me my ticket
and before I know I've done it I've rolled it up
and I'm sucking on it like a cigarette.
I hold it with my fingers.
I roll it.
I flick it.
I hold it in my lips.
But there's a snag with my bus ticket cigarettes:
they go soggy,
they go gooey
and I nibble
and I bite

and I chew –
my bus tickets get shorter and shorter
and before I know I've done it
all I've got is a bit of soggy paper
rolling round my mouth.
Disgusting.
Smokers buy pills to stop their filthy habit.
All I've got is bus inspectors.
You see, once, not long ago,
I was on a bus
and my ticket was in a ball
rolling round my mouth
and suddenly – above me –
there's the inspector.
'Tickets please' he says,
and there's me – nibble, nibble, nibble
on the mushed up ball of paper in my mouth.
He wants to see my ticket.
Of course he can see my ticket
if he doesn't mind inspecting a little ball of mush.
So I say, 'Yes, you can see my ticket,'
and I stuck my finger in my mouth
and hauled out the blob.
He looks at it.
He looks at me. It's sitting there on the end of my finger.
'What's that?' he says,
'My ticket,' I said,
'What did you have for breakfast?' he says,
'Corn Flakes', I said.
'Mmm,' he says,
'Did you ever think of having a slice or two of toast,
as well, old son' he says,
'and maybe you won't be so tempted by our tickets.'
And he left it at that.
But it's hard to break the habit,
even after a warning like that.
Got any ideas?

Smoke-loving girl blues by John Agard

Would like her for my girlfriend any day
Would follow if she showed the way
Would feel honoured if she be my queen

But she's a smoke-loving girl
And I'm allergic to nicotine

Would wheel with her on the ice-skating rink
Would fall with her over the brink
Would stare with her bewitched and serene

But she's a smoke-loving girl
And I'm allergic to nicotine

Would give her my last polo mint
Would hit the skies if she gave me a hint
Would do anything even dye my hair green

But she's a smoke-loving girl
And I'm allergic to nicotine

Would lay down my jacket for her gorgeous feet
Wouid fan her cheeks to keep away the heat
Would shine her shoes till she's lost in the sheen

But she's a smoke-loving girl
And I'm allergic to nicotine

Lawd now my head is in a haze
Cause of that girl and her smoke-loving ways

Poems suitable for conversation classes and creative writing

Poems with a story

Using stories
p 43

Example: *A bad habit*
Retell the story: put these events in the correct order as you listen to or read the poem:
The ticket inspector appeared.
He rolled his bus ticket up and smoked it.
He removed his ticket from his mouth.
He bought his bus ticket.
His ticket got smaller and wetter.
He showed his bus ticket to the inspector.
He started to eat and chew his ticket.
Retell the story to your partner using: firstly; next; then; so; and; but.

Example: *Smoke-loving girl blues*
Listen and make a list of all the things the poet is prepared to do for his love.
Give her the last of his favourite mint sweets, use his jacket, etc.
Compare notes in pairs and then listen/read again to complete your list.
'Would you be prepared to do these things for a person you love?'

Poems which introduce an issue can be a stimulus for discussion

Discussion on issues
pp 51–3

Examples:
Poem 1 *A bad habit* (bad habits)
Make a questionnaire to find out about bad habits in your class or students' attitudes towards smoking (at school, at home, in public places, with boyfriends/girlfriends). Interview a person from another group.

Ranking tasks for discussion
p 52

Poem 2 *Smoke-loving girl blues* (smoking)
Group discussion. *List three ways to give young people information about smoking. Give two examples of how you could encourage young people to give up smoking.*

Put these influences in order of importance: Who influences young people's habits most?
parents; peers (friends); teachers and school; television; magazines/newspapers; brothers/sisters

Poems with dialogue or characters: suitable for role play

Poem 1. In pairs, act out the dialogue between Mike and the ticket inspector.

Poem 2. In pairs, imagine the conversation between the boy and the smoke-loving girl when he asks her out.

Poem 2. Write a letter to the smoke-loving girl to tell her that you like her. Explain your feelings about smoking and suggest a date on condition that she either gives up or ...?

Two short poems on a similar theme which can be contrasted

Example tasks: Student A reads *A bad habit* and student B reads *Smoke-loving girl blues*. Put students in pairs and they tell each other the story or message in the poem. Then read or hear each others' poems. They can even read to each other in a good class. They then discuss in small groups which poem they like best. What are the reasons for liking a poem? Each group chooses their favourite and performs it as a group, each person reading a section or part. They can record themselves if time allows.

Note: All these activities are suitable for exploiting song lyrics and contrasting two songs on a theme.

Dialogue for role play
pp 44–5

Contrasting two photographs for fluency practice
pp 77–8

Useful tips – exploiting poems

- **If the poem is a springboard for speaking**, don't dwell in detail on every word and nuance.

- **Prepare vocabulary with a task before reading**. If the poem is too linguistically challenging you will get bogged down in vocabulary explanations during reading, e.g. look at the verbs in Poem 1: nibble, bite, chew (check in dictionaries and act them out), then read first to find out what does the poet chew?

- **Give students a task to access the meaning** of the poem quickly and to help them read it.

- **Encourage involvement and anticipation** by feeding the poem little by little, with questions for prediction at each stage. In Poem 1, stop the tape/reading when the Inspector approaches. *'What will Mike do?'* *'What will the inspector say?'* *'Will he throw Mike off the bus?'*

Pronunciation
of sounds
pp 56–63

- **Use it for speech work**. Decide if students are to hear the poem before they read. Will you involve the class in reading it aloud? Will you focus on intonation of questions or pronunciation of certain consonants and vowels? You could give key words on the board and students listen/read and complete. In poem two, focus on rhyme, similar vowel sounds; the /i/ in mint, brink, hint contrasted with the /iː/ in queen, green, sheen, feet, heat.

Speaking tasks
based on texts
pp 51–3

- **Have a concrete task for speaking** to follow up the poem. Dialogue building, guided discussion, group decision-making, role play.

- **Song lyrics can be treated as poems** and then the music introduced after you have exploited the poem. This can come as a nice surprise and avoids too much pressure to sing in an awkward class who don't like singing but like listening to music.

Newspapers and magazines

If you have chosen to use an article to get some conversation going then it should be short, easy to present and fairly straightforward. You need to get a summary of the main ideas quickly with a task and move on to your main speaking objective. Too often lessons with newspapers turn into reading lessons, rather than discussions.

Choosing texts for discussion pp 46–7

Example: An article from the *Daily Mail* on school uniforms (which can be used as a stimulus for fluency practice).

An article from the UK national press about school students excluded from school because they came to school in uniform skirts that were too short can be transformed into numerous situations for role play.

Situation 1: Re-enact the conversation between the headmistress/teacher and the pupil who has arrived unsuitably dressed.

Role play pp 44–5

Situation 2: You are the newspaper reporter who prepared this article. Interview one of the parents or students to find out what happened and what they think.

Exploit headlines

* Show headlines first and exploit them for speculation. Sub-headings (often used in magazines) can indicate the general content of the article and how its development is structured.

* Collect four or five headlines from short articles (six to eight lines long) and ask students to match them to three possible articles. The articles could be on related themes or even the same topic.

* Give a very short article (human interest) and get students to write the headline. Give out four different human interest articles with no headlines. Students in groups write a headline. Put up all headlines on the board. Mix up the articles and give them out again. Choose the headline from the board which suits your article.

Exploit all visual material

Visual aids
pp 68–79

Articles might have graphs or statistics. Don't just give them to students raw. Use them to generate language. When an American teen magazine published the results of a national survey on sex differences in education, the results were interesting. To involve students before seeing the results we need to engage them in prediction and in a personal way. A small graph can take up a whole lesson!

Task: Boys versus girls

Are these facts true?
Discuss in pairs/groups (preferably boys and girls mixed).

- Boys drop out of school more than girls.
- Boys talk earlier than girls.
- Girls learn to count earlier than boys.
- Boys are more likely to go to university than girls.
- Girls prefer to read more novels than boys.
- Girls are better at writing than boys.
- Boys are more interested in languages than girls.

Look at the statistics. Are you surprised? Modify the statements to make them reflect the survey results. Make a list of four statements about young people in your country. Does everyone in your group agree?

**The students'
own culture**
p 110

**Personalising
topics**
p 52

Dealing with vocabulary

Grading tasks –
getting the level right
pp 81–3

Always anticipate vocabulary problems and provide tasks to do before and during reading. However, if the percentage of new words means that students struggle through each paragraph, there will be little room for discussion or enjoyment, and students will feel disheartened, no matter how interesting the topic.

> ## *Vocabulary tasks*
>
> ### Matching
> After eliciting vocabulary related to the topic by giving headlines or key words, give definitions for key items in the article. Students read through and match the definition to the word
>
> ### Finding synonyms and offering antonyms
> Provide a short list of synonyms for an article and students find those words in the article with a similar meaning. Offer an antonym, e.g. not polite = rude, when a synonym is not possible.
>
> ### Contextual guess work
> Give two possible explanations for an item in the text and students use the situation to guess the most likely meaning of the word from the ones offered. A native teacher might provide two possible translations but beware of getting into deep water if you try the same!
>
> ### Using dictionaries
> If your students are more advanced but still using bilingual dictionaries, using a monolingual dictionary could be a new skill they acquire with you. Helping themselves to deal with real newspapers should be your aim.

Unit 12 Building a resource bank

Before leaving the UK

It is difficult to predict exactly what you will need in your host school but there are certain basic materials that are helpful in most language teaching situations. Try to get as much idea of the standard of English in your school before leaving as you can consult relevant textbooks and teaching material at ELT bookshops and university libraries. It is unwise to buy piles of books only to find that they don't suit the age range and language levels of the students. Invest in one or two basic reference works, like a good grammar of English for language teachers, but hold back on any purchases if you are not clear about your future teaching situation. However, a basic store of visuals and authentic materials should be collected before you leave the UK.

- **Start with yourself**. Collect photos of your family, pets, home, living environment, friends, holidays and town. Focus on photos of people doing everyday things, families at festival times, spare-time activities, etc.

- **Look for material in English about your host country**, such as tourist brochures advertising holidays to the region. If you are aware of the school type and know you will use newspaper articles, start collecting articles about your host country too. Obviously avoid anything too topical that might date. Short articles rather than detailed analysis will be best. Find advertisements for products from the host country. How are these products sold to English people? What image is created of their country? Is it a stereotyped view? These types of material are useful for cultural studies.

- **Make your own personal tape** (or even video if you have the equipment). Record a range of people speaking clearly and in an interesting way about their likes/dislikes, everyday routines, jobs, family, holidays, etc. Interview friends and family. These interviews and recordings should be easily divided into short sections of one to three minutes. You may even find someone who has visited or lived in your host country to talk about their experience.

- **Make a songs (or poetry) cassette**. Record suitable songs from your collection, including two or three recent hits, but try to avoid things that will date. Remember to focus mainly on clear singing without too much background noise and clearly enunciated lyrics. Check on websites and in song books at your library. Some modern EFL courses have songs as part of the course, so if you can consult books check what those songs are and how they are exploited. Use friends and family to record a selection of poetry from an anthology aimed at the age range you will be teaching. GCSE and AS level anthologies will give you ideas.

Using local resources in your host country

It will be easy to supplement your picture collection by using the same procedures as below, getting magazines locally if necessary. Make use of maps of the town where you are staying and leaflets in English (if the English is correct) since students can always play themselves helping a tourist in their own country. This is also the most likely scenario as many may meet foreigners on their own territory and have to give directions, give help at the station or explain dishes on a menu. Some students in upper secondary, especially tourism and commercial schools, need to practise more specific situations linked to industry and contacts in their area. Discuss this with teachers in these types of school. Use leaflets and situations from local *bureaux de change*, hotels, industries or tourist attractions.

Visual aids

Realia/props

Collect as much authentic material as you can before leaving the UK. There's nothing more immediate than holding the real thing. Pick up a few copies if you can as it will save on photocopying.

- Collect pub menus, menus from cafés, restaurants and fast food places.

- Bus or train timetables, information leaflets, instructions for using the phone to call abroad or leaflets from post offices, banks and libraries can all be useful.

- Greetings cards, postcards and invitations can be a good source of language and stimulus for discussion. Build up a theme, e.g. postcards of places, people, funny postcards, works of art, greetings cards for festivals, for family events or for everyday celebrations like passing an exam, moving house, etc. Ask family and friends for cards they don't want.

- Leaflets from local theatres, cinemas, concert halls or advertisements from events and listings magazines may form the basis of speaking and reading activities.

Visual aids
pp 68–79

Ways of introducing a cultural topic
pp 103–5

Collecting and storing pictures for flashcards

Controlled oral practice
pp 37–41

- Collect pictures from magazines in categories, e.g. food, hobbies, clothes, everyday activities, or broader discussion themes like the environment, cultural activities, teenage life, crime, education or immigration.

- Stick pictures on card, cover with plastic if possible, and store them in groups with notes on what type of language they might 'generate'. For example, divide your food and drink pictures into countable/uncountable nouns.

- Pictures can be collected to practise structures, language functions or vocabulary areas. Make a note of this as you collect. For example, for the function of making/accepting invitations, collect a series of pictures of places to invite someone to, like a cinema, a party, a swimming pool, a game of tennis, etc.

Sources of pictures

Before buying lots of magazines explore ways of getting free magazines for building up your collection.

Using photos
pp 77–8

- Ask all friends and family for magazines, Sunday supplements, television magazines, holiday brochures, supermarket publicity and mail order catalogues. Just three or four of those small mail order catalogues free with Sunday supplements and women's magazines will give you a good collection of household objects to cut up and make into card games for a whole class. You should be looking for variety and quantity and a good range of unusual and large photographs for stimulating discussion.

Using card games
pp 95–6

- Collect a variety of holiday brochures from travel agents to have a wealth of flashcard images and small card images for locations, climate, activities, monuments and much more.

- Find pictures of key UK and American figures (not just fleetingly famous), big enough for flashcards, such as members of the Royal Family, the prime minister, personalities in international sport or music, etc. Add local figures once you arrive in your host country.

Using advertisements
p 78

- Collect advertisements which can be grouped by product type or advertisements aimed at young people. Look for issues that would appeal to young people, such as anti-drugs advertisements, advertisements for slimming products, alcohol, fashion, etc.

Posters or maps

You can get free posters from local tourist boards. There are also very cheap ranges of posters sold in local libraries in the UK which can be particularly useful for younger learners, such as weather, shapes, or counting posters. Large organisations also give schools posters (see cultural resources).

Useful maps and wall-charts

• A map of the UK, your region or your town. Small maps of local areas of interest or the town centre (maybe maps of the local transport network) can be useful for information gap activities and role plays.

• Maps of the UK in geography or history books often show specific features, such as the spread of industry, the different climatic conditions or the concentrations of population. Maps of this sort are useful for your Cultural Studies lessons as you can write questions based on the maps and discuss the country using this visual stimulus.

• Make your own posters about the UK based on these small maps if and when you need them. The advantage of posters is that they are easy to roll up and transport and can be adapted to all your classes.

• Free wall-charts from national organisations are good for vocabulary and Cultural Studies (see below).

Pictures and cartoons for describing and story telling

You have to be careful with cartoons as it could be assumed that they are easy when in fact they often contain a great deal of culture-specific reference. Cartoons in newspapers can refer to a topic in the news at the moment or a trend unknown to students, and may use colloquial language unfamiliar to students. Choose carefully to find short strip cartoons for story telling, reordering, dialogue building and discussion. Individual cartoon pictures can work well, e.g. the work of Gary Larson in *The Far Side* can sometimes provide an interesting and amusing starting point for a theme.

Games and communication activities

Use board games (e.g. Scrabble), memory games and game props (e.g. dice). Puzzle books, holiday books and quiz books for young people. These are an excellent source of word mazes, spot the difference pictures, join the dots, and pictures for describing as well as teasers which activate language. For example, a puzzle book for Christmas might have anagrams for Christmas words hidden in

Exploiting cultural content
pp 106–9

Introducing cultural topics
pp 103–5

Tasks for picture stories
p 76

Changes of pace
pp 17–18

Choosing cultural topics for learners
p 112

a picture, or a holiday book may have a crossword which can be adapted or used with classes. Even if written for native speakers, they can be a good source of games and five-minute filler activities for language learners. Check out children's and teen sites on the Internet, especially sites relating to celebrations like Easter or Halloween in the UK.

Fig. 1 **Basic pronunciation table**

Problems	German speakers	French speakers	Spanish speakers
Consonants	/θ/ (think) and /ð/ (these) do not occur in German. /w/ (window) is a problem sound as learners may confuse with /v/ or /f/. /b/, /d/ and /g/ are sounds which cause difficulty at the end of a word and tend to be substituted by /p/, /t/ and /k/.	/θ/ (think) and /ð/ (these) do not occur in French. /s/ tends to be substituted by /z/. /tʃ/ and /dʒ/ (jam) do not occur in French. /ŋ/ (sing) does not occur in French. /h/ is often omitted and inserted when it shouldn't be.	/b/ (boat) and /v/ (vote) are confused and tend to be substituted by a combination of the two. /j/ (year) tends to be substituted by /dʒ/ (jeer). /θ/ (thought) is often substituted by /f/ (fought) or /s/ (sought). /ʃ/ (shoe) does not occur in Spanish. /h/ is often omitted, or conversely, over-pronounced.
Vowels	/ɒ/ (hot) can be a problem. /a/ (bad) can be confused with /ɛ/ (bed). /ʌ/ (fun) does not occur in German.	/ɪ/ (ship) and /i/ (sheep) are confused as /ɪ/ does not occur in French. Learners use /i/ for both. /a/ (bad) and /ʌ/ (fun) are often confused.	/ɪ/ (ship) and /i/ (sheep) are confused as /ɪ/ does not occur in Spanish. Learners use /i/ for both. There is no weakening of vowels, so /ə/ (the schwa) will be problematic. /a/ (bad) can be confused with /ɛ/ (bed). Vowels tend to be pronounced phonetically.
Rhythm	The rhythm of German is very similar to that of English, so there shouldn't be too many problems.	The rhythm of French is very different from that of English. Learners need to focus on reduced vowels in unstressed syllables.	Each syllable in Spanish is pronounced very clearly with a full vowel. This is often transferred to English.
Word stress	In German there are strong and weak forms of words, but attention should be drawn to weak forms in English.	English words have a tendency for stress to fall at the front of words whereas in French it tends to be at the end. The mobility of stress in English words is problematic, especially when the stress falls on the first syllable.	Compound nouns (such as download) are a problem as Spanish has no equivalent, so all parts are stressed.

Pronunciation

The table on page 130 outlines the main problem areas for speakers of French, German and Spanish. Use this as a reference guide when planning pronunciation work and building materials, such as cards to represent minimal pairs of sounds.

Finding texts for speaking and writing practice

Use the age range as your starting point. What type of reading material and content appeals to the age range in the UK? Look at teenage publications, at reading material in libraries, short story collections, poetry anthologies and popular music which appeals to this group of learners. Look at teenage publications on arrival in your host country too for topic ideas.

Speech work
pp 56–65

• Collect UK magazines for the age range you are going to teach. Apart from articles and stories, students also like to see and handle a whole magazine. Practise finding your way around a complete publication. These magazines can also be a good source of questionnaires to use for speaking or for short articles which can be used to stimulate discussion or used for dictation.

Example: *'It happened to me ... '. 'My worst ever holiday ...' 'I'll never forget when ...'* are common themes.

Problem pages, questionnaires and small advertisements all provide springboards for controlled and free speaking practice. Articles where three or four teenagers give their point of view on an issue can be useful, or articles where three or four products or people are being compared can generate a whole series of discussion tasks and language practice.

• Look out in the national press for articles that would appeal to the age range and could introduce an issue or topic. Special sections relevant to young people and the secondary curriculum can provide a good source, e.g. the section in the *Education Guardian* for schools with readings and web links. Also look for short human interest articles of five to ten lines for text dictations, reconstruction and discussion starters.

Motivating teenagers
pp 24–5

• Very short stories which are amusing, mysterious or thought-provoking. Find these in cheap collections like *Amazing but true* types of books and the non-fiction sections for young people in local libraries.

Discussion tasks
pp 51–3

• Magazines especially written for language learners can be an excellent source of texts from age eleven up to very advanced older teenage learners. Each country has a crop of these magazines. The most widely used and respected in Europe are the series published by Mary Glasgow International which contain activity pages that can be used in class. These magazines are also a good source of Cultural Studies material that is up to date and topical.

Cultural Studies resources

Using newspapers
pp 123

• **The press**. Start by looking at your daily paper from a foreigner's viewpoint. What can you learn about the latest social trends, what is the attitude towards issues and what can you find out about ordinary people, ethnic minorities or national institutions? Collect articles which will help introduce topics about your country and its people. Gather a good selection of papers to take which reflect the diversity of the British press, including Asian papers, papers for the Black community or specific religious communities. The UK is unique in the plurality of its press and the importance which it places on the written word.

• **National organisations**. Many national organisations provide an educational resource service for teachers. Posters, fact sheets and leaflets are often obtainable free by writing or visiting websites. The Parliamentary Education Unit has a website which will give you ideas and can be used by your students. Other types of organisation include national tourist boards, the Health Education Authority, the Commonwealth Institute, conservation organisations like the National Trust, youth organisations, large companies like Tesco (see their Tesco 2000 website) or charities. Local libraries can give you a list of addresses or websites to get you started.

• **Films, video, television and radio** reflect lifestyle, trends and attitudes and can be exploited for this.

• **Your own souvenirs and realia**. Recipes, local traditions and souvenirs from your area.

• **The media in your host country**. Capitalise on news stories as they occur, to give background, e.g. during elections, cover the system of government, during a crisis look at the issues. Refer to local media coverage of your country. It may be biased but you can redress that.

The Internet

You can visit the UK from your host country and follow events, lifestyle changes and festivals as they happen. Authentic material and statistics are easily obtainable and specific teaching resources for EFL and Cultural Studies are widely available. There are vast banks of educational material in all English-speaking countries to suit the age ranges you teach, and worksheets, visuals, texts and lesson plans can be downloaded. Here is a brief summary of possible resources for assistants. Selected links are provided on the Language**Assistant** website at *www.britishcouncil.org/languageassistant*

Websites for teachers and learners of EFL

You may wish to visit the British Council's Learn English site (*www.britishcouncil.org/learnenglish*) or the BBC's site for foreign learners, which has a good literature section (*www.bbc.co.uk/learningenglish*). Visiting main organisations in the field, such as IATEFL (*www.iatefl.org*) or TESOL (*www.tesol.org*) will give you links to more sites. The British Council also provides a useful site for teachers, which has lesson plans and teaching tips at *www.teachingenglish.org.uk*

Educational networks for secondary and primary schools

UK networks, including the BBC learning zone (*www.bbc.co.uk/learningzone*) and the National Grid for Learning (*www.ngfl.gov.uk*) are both rich sources of texts and writings by real teenagers. Canada and Australia have well-developed networks such as *www.schoolnet.ca* and *www.edunetconnect.com* for many issue-based lessons and international topics. Australia's cultural network is at *www.acn.net.au/culture*

School networks and websites

All English-speaking countries have links between schools who share learning resources and many schools have their own websites so you can visit a real elementary school from Canada to New Zealand and even e-mail the teachers and students. The school where you take up your placement might welcome the opportunity to link up with a UK school. School linking is provided as a service by the Global Gateway website – *www.globalgateway.org*. Schools from anywhere in the world can register and post a message about the projects they'd like to do and the exchanges they'd like to make. There are thousands of UK schools interested in partnering. You'll also find lots of ideas for education with an international dimension on the site.

Homework sites

Many English-speaking children use the Internet for their homework and these resources are also useful for language teachers. Try some of these examples and search for more on our Weblinks page *(www.britishcouncil.org/languageassistant-arc-weblinks.htm)*.

www.factmonster.com
www.webenglishteacher.com
www.elllo.org
www.usingenglish.com/handouts/index.php

Media sites

All major magazines and newspapers have their own young people's versions and sites linked to television (see the BBC's), which are a good source.

www.telegraph.co.uk
www.timeforkids.com

Media for teachers are also good for links to educational resources, e.g. www.tes.co.uk (The *Times Educational Supplement* online version).

National institutions

All have their own sites, which have educational sections with worksheets and resources aimed at schoolchildren. Examples include:

www.csu.edu.au/australia – comprehensive Australian government site for history, travel, geography

www. explore.parliament.uk – a schools guide to the system of government in the UK

www.royal.gov.uk – the official site of the British monarchy

International institutions

Official bodies like the United Nations and the Worldwide Fund for Nature have activities in English geared to children and schools: *www.wwf.org*

Electronic libraries and encyclopaedias

Far more fun because interactive, so bringing any topic alive, e.g.
www.spartacus.schoolnet.co.uk

Museums

There is a rich educational resource geared even to pre-school children in places like London's Natural History Museum where children can see dinosaurs in action, travel with Captain Cook on his journey to discover Australia and much, much more. *www.nhm.ac.uk/*

Published resources

Resources for games

Elementary communication games – Jill Hadfield (Longman ELT)
Photocopiable resource of pair and group games featuring role cards, picture prompts and information gap. Excellent for low levels. Also see Intermediate and Advanced versions in this series.

Play games with English (series of levels) – Colin Granger (Macmillan Heinemann ELT)
Small handbooks of filler activities for all classes.

Word games with English (series of levels) – Howard-Williams and Herd (Macmillan Heinemann ELT)

English puzzles (series of levels) – Doug Case (Macmillan Heinemann ELT)

Beginners – Peter Grundy (Oxford University Press)
has lots of suggestions for activities.

Games for Children – Gordon Lewis and Gunther Bedson (Oxford University Press)
has a collection of games for four- to twelve-year-olds.

The grammar activity book – Bob Obee (Cambridge University Press)
From elementary to upper-intermediate. Contains over sixty ready-to-use, photocopiable grammar games for younger/teenage learners.

Grammar games – Mario Rinvolucri (Cambridge University Press)

Grammar in action again – Christine Frank and Mario Rinvolucri (Prentice Hall)

Grammar games and *Vocabulary games* – Peter Watcyn-Jones (Penguin ELT)

Grammar Dictation – Ruth Wajnryb improves understanding of grammar through reconstruction of texts.

Basic reference material (essential for all assistants)

A good monolingual dictionary for language teaching that you can refer to in class, e.g. the *COBUILD Essential English dictionary* (Collins) is good for classroom use as it gives examples in context, which are helpful in lessons, rather than just a basic definition.

The *Cambridge learner's dictionary* is good for intermediate learners upwards.

A grammar reference that helps you think of your language from a learner's point of view, such as *Practical English usage* – Michael Swan (OUP)

Recommended resources and background reading for visuals

1,000 pictures for teachers to copy – Andrew Wright (Longman ELT)
A very useful book for copying drawings for the blackboard and finding pictures for composition and eliciting key vocabulary and structures. It contains useful hints on using pictures for language teaching.

Visuals for the language classroom – Wright and Haleem (Longman ELT)

Visual impact – D.A. Hill (Longman)

Recommended resources for speaking activities

Conversation – Rob Nolasco and Lois Arthur (Oxford University press) has lots of ideas to motivate speaking.

Keep Talking – Friederike Klippel (Cambridge University Press) has communicative fluency activities that involve little or no preparation.

Pronunciation and speech work resources

Pronunciation games – Mark Hancock (CUP)
Good for raising awareness, controlled practice and revision.

Teaching English pronunciation – Joanne Kenworthy (Longman)

Ship or sheep? and *Tree or three?* – Ann Baker (CUP)

Conversation – Rob Nolasco (OUP)

Keep talking – Friederike Klippel (CUP)
Fluency activities, useful for higher levels.

Discussions that work – Penny Ur (CUP)
Ways to get students talking.

Sources for dictation

Dictation – Paul Davis and Mario Rinvolucri (CUP)
Ground-breaking look at new and creative ways to use dictation in ELT.

General methodology and guidelines

The source book – Michael Lewis and Jimmie Hill (Macmillan Heinemann ELT)
A practical introduction to work as an assistant.

Learning teaching – Jim Scrivener (Macmillan Heinemann ELT)
Useful for assistants who find themselves teaching whole classes alone.

Literature in ELT resources

Literature in the language classroom – Joanne Collie and Stephen Slater (OUP)

A window on literature (Literary extracts for lower-intermediate learners) – Gillian Lazar (CUP)

Literature – Alan Duff and Alan Maley (OUP)